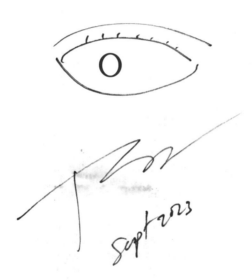

Sept 2023

ISBN 978-1-946433-91-6
First Edition, First Printing, 2022
750 copies

Ugly Duckling Presse
The Old American Can Factory
232 Third Street #E-303
Brooklyn, NY 11215
www.uglyducklingpresse.org

Distributed in the USA by SPD/Small Press Distribution
Distributed in the UK by Inpress Books

Artwork and calligraphy by Tammy Nguyen
Design and typesetting by wrongfoot and Sonya Bui
The type is Vendome

Printed and bound at McNaughton & Gunn
Covers printed offset by Prestige Printing and letterpress at UDP
Inserts printed by Linco Printing and die-cut by Tammy Nguyen
Inserts tipped in and holes punched by volunteers at UDP

"Call to the Youths" translation by Lena Bui, reproduced with permission.
Constitutional articles excerpted from constituteproject.org's *Viet Nam's Constitution of 1992 with Amendments through 2013*, prepared from texts collected in International IDEA's ConstitutionNet.

The publication of this book was made possible, in part, by public funds from the New York City Department of Cultural Affairs in partnership with the City Council, and by the continued support of the New York State Council on the Arts with the support of the Office of the Governor and the New York State Legislature.
This project is supported by the Robert Rauschenberg Foundation.

TAMMY NGUYEN

O

SEEN LIBRARY

LOS ANGELES, C

FOR MY UNCLE, VÕ VĂN NHỰT

"O-O-O-O-O-O-O-O," I gurgled from the back of my throat. Dr. Don poked his circular mirror around in my mouth. In another mirror that I had been given to hold, I watched him probe my upper gums. Then, in his black, disc-like spinning chair, he pirouetted over to his desk and grabbed my x-rays. "We will have to figure out what to do with you," he said.

I was eight, lying on the dentist's chair, staring up at the round and blinding operatory lights. Minutes earlier, I had heard Mrs. Nguyễn cry from the other room: "We must help her!"

My x-rays had just been processed. They showed evidence of a birth defect known as congenitally missing lateral incisors: quite simply, two of my front teeth did not exist. Just one week earlier, on the playground, I had been picking at my baby incisors, noodling my tongue around them and peeling them slowly away from my gums. They were the last of my baby teeth; I was getting excited for my permanent smile. But upon learning that my smile would be abnormal, my excitement turned to confusion and anxiety.

"The teeth you just lost will not be coming back in," Dr. Don continued, pleasant and matter-of-fact. "Some people, like your mother, have very thin incisors, but you don't have them at all. But it's not uncommon. Some people let their teeth naturally fill in the empty spaces so their canines sit next to their front teeth. Others push the canines back to make room for false lateral incisors. You know, we don't need these teeth anymore, and someday, no one will have them. You might just be ahead of human evolution!"

Four hundred million years ago, rain fell on Gondwana and eroded the limestone in the Earth. The land shifted. Wind pattered, slapped, and whipped, boring into the hollows of the stone, pushing the water ahead of it and sculpting the rock into an ecosystem of caves. For hundreds of millions of years, countless species have thrived in the places where the meeting of acidic water and corrosive rock had created a matrix of riverways.

The Phong Nha Karst is located in the Annamite Mountains, which spread across the borders of Vietnam, Laos, and Cambodia. "Phong" is a Vietnamese word derived from the Chinese—"fung" in Cantonese or "feng" in Mandarin— for "wind." "Nha" is Vietnamese for "teeth," though it is more commonly combined with other words to describe things related to teeth. For example, "Nha sĩ" means dentist; "Nha khoa" means "dentistry." According to Chinese mythology, the ridges of the Phong Nha Karst are the Earth's teeth, carved by wind.

Vietnam adopted a new constitution in 1992. After the fall of the Soviet Union, decades of economic isolation, and in the wake of the Đổi Mới reform movements that began in 1986, a series of constitutional amendments reintroduced Vietnam on the global stage. The new constitution reduced the powers of the Vietnamese Communist Party and defined new forms of ownership; individuals, private companies, and foreign investors could now lease land for decades.

In the same year, a former farmer in China, Yang Guoqiang, created a company called Country Garden—a real estate development firm that, decades later, would change the shape of land in Asia.

Also that year, Hồ Khanh, another farmer who lived in Phong Nha, wanted to seek shelter from the rain. He found a hole in the side of a cliff and crawled in, only to find that the hole was endless. He kept crawling.

In an ancient time, three prisoners were chained inside a cave in such a way that they could only see the cave's inner wall. There was a fire burning behind them, and behind that fire was the cave's mouth. As people and animals passed by, the light of the sun would cast their shadows onto the back wall. The only thing the prisoners could see were these shadows, and they would play a game with each other, attempting to guess what shadow would pass next. Whoever guessed correctly would receive praise from the others and be deemed, for a time, the Master of Nature.

This continued until the day one prisoner broke free. Leaving his chains, he went out of the cave and discovered the world outside. He was bewildered by the objects and people now surrounding him. He discovered the sun and named it the source of all truth. He decided his former life—sitting in the cave, looking at the shadows, and playing the guessing game— had been pointless and false.

He returned to the cave and told the other prisoners what he had discovered. Enraged, they threatened to kill him.

My uncle was born Võ Văn Nhựt. Everyone in the Chợ Cây Quéo neighborhood of Sài Gòn agreed: he was the most handsome man in the area. Tall and broad-shouldered, he kept a muscular physique and carried himself with a macho confidence. The beauty that others saw in him, he also demanded; he associated beauty with wealth and wealth with success. He expected high noses, fit bodies, and—his biggest fixation—glowing, straight-toothed smiles.

In the sixties, my uncle became a pilot for the South Vietnamese Air Force, which sent him to Texas to train. This may have been when he decided that America possessed the most beauty, wealth, and success of any country on Earth. He became a successful businessman in the seventies, after he was released from duty. Seeded with Western ambition, he began exporting Vietnamese porcelain for a company in Florida. Back and forth he went, pushing empty vessels from Vietnam in the land of dreams. He pushed so many vessels that he was able to build one for himself, in the form of a giant French colonial style house for his mother and ten siblings.

In 1972, David Van created a shell company that claimed to import and export ceramics from Vietnam. This pretense allowed him to come to Florida, only to ditch the balmy beaches for the arid desert of Reno, Nevada. Under a sublime sun, the Sierra Nevada Mountains infused him with a motivation he had never felt before. Sporting a tough, squeaky leather jacket in his Chevrolet Chevelle, he cruised the wide highways of Nevada, looking for a permanent path in America.

It didn't take long for him to map his road by way of a Vietnamese woman, already a US citizen, named Maria. My uncle married her in 1976, and together they ran a nail salon in Reno, where they tended to the aesthetic needs of women and their own appetite for the casinos. It must have been around this time that he changed his name to David Van—David, for the David who fought Goliath, and Van, extracted from his real middle name, meant to make his new American name sound a little Dutch.

By 1980, the nail salon had become tiresome and the marriage had lost its luster, so David Van cashed in all of his savings to score a taxi medallion in San Francisco. That piece of metal would soon make him millions. He leased it out to other drivers at inflated rates that started to earn him a reputation, particularly among the Vietnamese drivers: my uncle was a crooked dude.

Despite my father's hesitation about David Van, my mother loved him, and he became a fixture in my daily life around 1992, when I was eight and his life had collapsed. By then he had three ex-wives; an abandoned business, with the first; a disowned child, from the second; and two more kids, who left with their mother, from the third.

Alone, he came to our house for dinner several times a week. He would tell long yarns about this person and that person, pounding his fist passionately on my parents' oak dining table. He'd be wearing a short-sleeved polo, his left tricep flexing beneath it each time his clenched fist hit the surface of the table. Seated directly across from him, I would watch the gorgeous American eagle tattoo that wrapped around his upper arm. The fierce bird of prey spread its wings slightly upward. Both claws clutched the pole of an American flag as the banner waved behind its body. The ink of the tattoo had blended and faded to a peaceful greenish-grey color. It really seemed to be a part of my uncle's skin; as his tricep pulsed, the eagle and the American flag pulsed with it.

After dinner, my parents and David Van stayed up for hours watching *Paris by Night* videos. In these highly-produced concerts, Vietnamese entertainers of the war diaspora would sing and dance to traditional music and contemporary pop tunes. Sitting back in the recliner with a grin on his face, still clenching his fists, my uncle would point out which performers had veneers, which had implants, and which had natural teeth.

"Teeth are everything," David Van advised my parents. "The Americans take you seriously when you have a nice set of teeth. It doesn't matter how smart you are—if you have a good face with nice, straight white teeth, people will take you seriously in this country. You'd better take her to see the orthodontist."

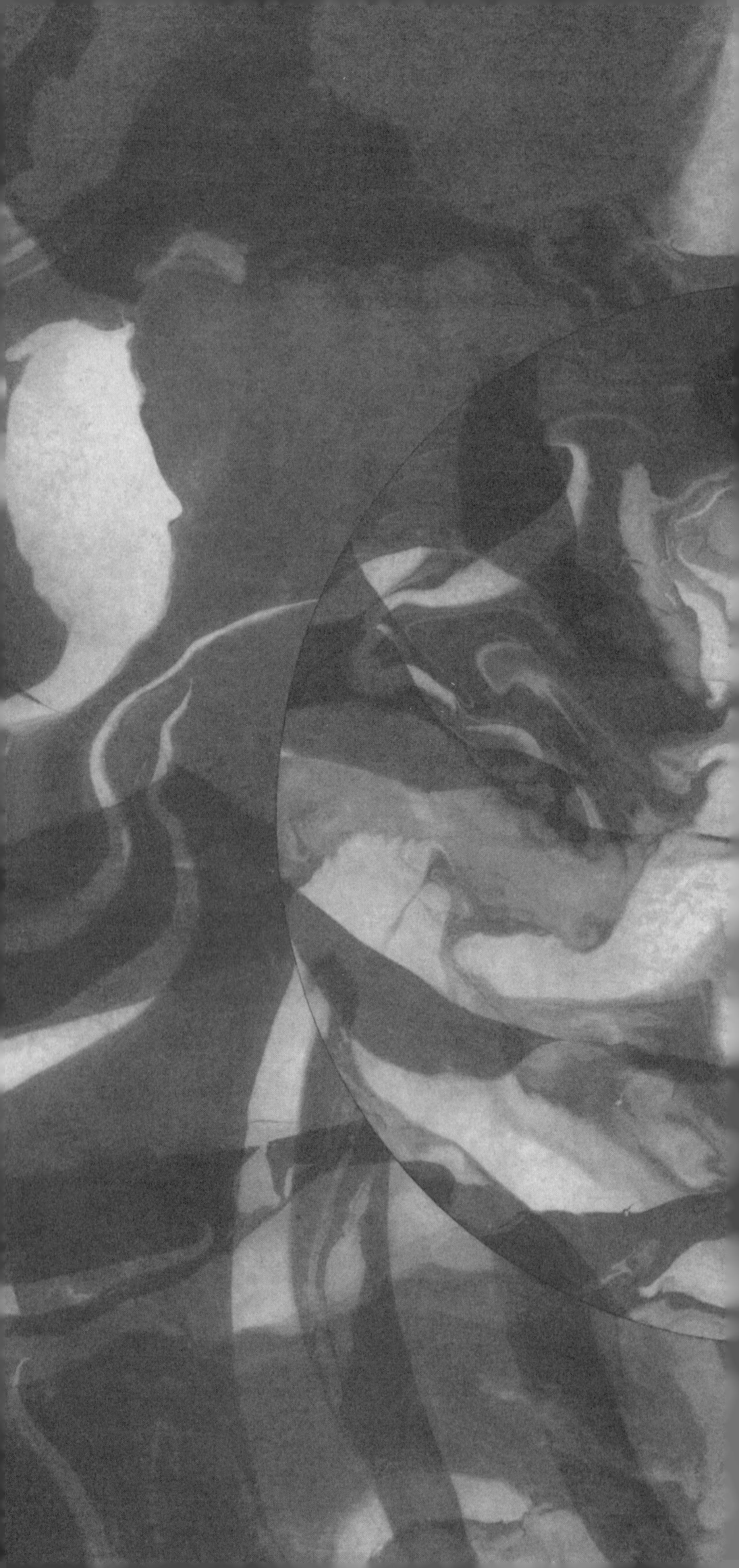

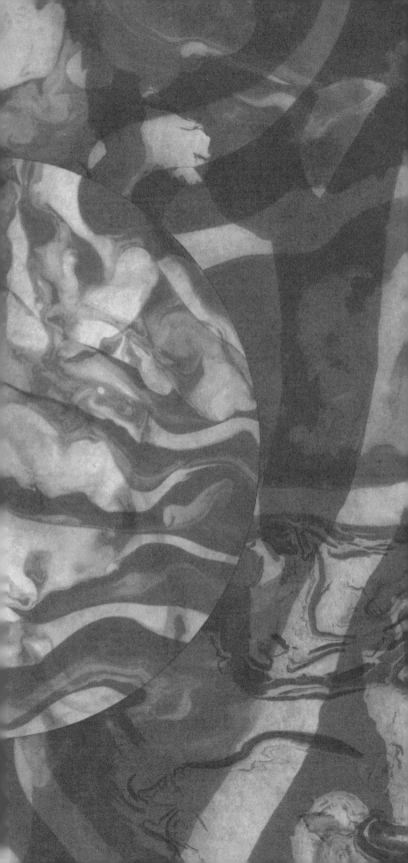

His own teeth were perfect and, I always assumed, natural. It was not until years later that my father told me that my uncle's perfect smile, just like his nose and eyelids, was fake.

When Yang Guoqiang was 10, he was working on a farm barefoot in Foshan, a town in Guangdong Province, China. He didn't receive his first pair of shoes until he was 18. But even as a child, he could feel that modernity was coming to China—that his suburban town would one day glisten with glass buildings, their yards landscaped with manicured flowers and exotic plants.

In 1978, Yang left the agrarian pastures of his childhood to work for Shundee Beijiao Development, a company in his hometown, where he rose quickly through the ranks. At Shundee, he saw how a strong and fluid infrastructure was integral to the growth of a company, and how honoring hierarchies was key to simultaneously maintaining oversight and trust. These lessons became the foundation for Yang's own company, now famously known as Country Garden, which he started and headquartered in Foshan—right on the land that he had farmed as a young boy.

"I can still build a house with my bare hands," Yang says, decades later. Today, his company has redefined the Foshan skyline with modern high rises. Since its incorporation in 1992, Country Garden has undertaken more than 500 projects in over 300 cities, housing more than three million people. As of 2019, its total revenue stands at over $70 billion.

We were on our way to Phong Nha–Kẻ
Bàng National Forest to see the caves.
While still on the road, a brightness
through the car window stung my eyes
open. We were surrounded by glorious
mountains and luscious rice paddies. The
rolling flora felt ancestral, as if the ancient
hills and rivers, passed down from our
fathers, had been opened to us. Miles of
rice paddies surrounded the mountains
like a carpet, or a grand driveway, or
the gigantic lawn meant to emphasize
the importance of a palace. The rice
paddies glistened electric green, a hue you
might see at a nightclub or painted on a
Lamborghini. It was strange to see such a
green in nature.

From a distance, it is impossible to
know which mountains are caves, which
geological formations are rock and which
are hollow. It wasn't until we came upon
a lagoon that I saw the cave's opening.
I could hear water splashing, children
laughing, and shuffling footsteps. When
I followed the sounds of glee back to
their source, I saw that from another
promontory people were jumping off of

zip lines, laughing carefree; beneath them, others were paddling canoes.

To get inside the cave, we had to enter as if we were Tarzan: riding the longest zipline in Asia, 400 meters from one side of the lagoon straight into its yawning mouth. "𝒪-𝒪-𝒪-𝒪-𝒪-𝒪-𝒪-𝒪," one tourist, and then another, and then another flew down the zipline. The speed down the line was sensational. I could feel the whole weight of my body strain my triceps. Gushes of air rushed into my mouth and bubbled in my cheeks. I tried to keep my eyes open to see the landing, but the speed smeared the tropical scenes into indistinguishable streaks of blue and green. Before I could find my composure, my feet skidded onto a landing mat splayed over a flat rock. I had arrived at the mouth of the cave.

My husband was already waiting for me, along with other members of our tour group: a German family of four and a young Dutch couple, both dentists. Our guide, Đông, was also waiting; he had lived in Quảng Bình his whole life.

"Welcome to the home of King Kong!" Đông began. In 2016, he explained,

Warner Brothers, Legendary Entertainment, and Tencent Productions brought the $185-million-dollar *Kong: Skull Island* production to Quang Bình. Tzzhey set King Kong's birthplace in the exact area of Phong Nha that we would be exploring. "They shut down this whole area for weeks," said Dong, who then took out his iPhone to show us an online promotional spot of the film's director Jordan Vogt-Roberts praising the region's beauty over a soundtrack of Hollywood adventure music. "I kept asking, do people understand how beautiful this is?" Vogt-Roberts asked. "To me, it's so otherworldly and spectacular, and it's just the daily life of other people. I hope that they realize how special the place that they live in is."

We followed Dong into the cave. Once we were inside the mouth of the mountain, modernity went silent. The cave air was refreshing—clean and pure, free from the smog that is ubiquitous in Vietnam—but it had a particulate wetness to it, too; it was as thick and as dense as the inside of a mouth. Breathing required an adjustment. The wind was unpredictable: warm air blowing in from the lagoon was accented by cold gusts that came from deeper within the cave. "Go forth with the wind," directed Đồng, confusingly. As we moved into the cave's throat, we learned to follow the wind's warmth. It became one way for us to navigate into the darkness.

Above our heads, cones of dripping rock hung like candle wax. To our sides, geological slabs were stacked like boulder-sized books of knowledge. The ground below shimmered in tiny planes of limestone, salt, and the silver-and-gold glitter of gypsum. When I turned to look back, the water running into the cave glowed like tonic water in black light. It was refreshing—pristine and seemingly untouched, even though the whole setup had been engineered for our enjoyment.

Because the cave mouth provided the main source of natural light, the cave darkened quickly and dramatically the deeper we went. There were eight of us in the tour group; as the cave swallowed us, our eyes filled with wonder. We looked up and around. Our headlights winked against the geological formations, performing a kind of dance of shadows and stars. Dwindling natural light cast shadows on protruding rock ridges, theater curtains for some primordial play.

As we continued, tall rocks rose like large white tree trunks holding up the vessel's dome. We approached a small, steep slope and climbed down carefully, our legs' triangular movements conforming to the treacherous surface of the rock. At the bottom, we found a small beach. A porter ushered us into a stream of water. Here, the ground no longer seemed like a ground at all. Just as the roof above and walls around us were pocketed with hidden cavities, the floor beneath the murky water was riddled with deep, cylindrical holes, some almost three feet deep. Walking through this water, the notion of a ground at all began to seem arbitrary: it seemed, instead, that the cave was just one big tube of rock and cavities, and we just happened to be scaling the side to which gravity had chosen to anchor itself.

Our group of eight was quiet. All we could hear was the sound of dripping water. Every once in a while, someone

would gasp from a sudden trip or fall.
The cave walls narrowed and narrowed
until we were walking in single file:
O- O- O -O -O -O- O-O. The water beneath
us became deeper and thicker. Before we
knew it, we found ourselves submerged
in a natural mud bath. Our bodies rose to
the top of the muddy pond at the heart of
the cavern's hollow.

Đông laughed. "It is good for your
skin!" The water was so thick with
sediment that none of us could actually
sit down to bathe. Some of us giggled
as we fought the buoyancy of the water.
Others tried to work with it and float. As
we played, our bodies projected shadows
on the limestone walls of the cavern. You
could make up whole tales about the
shadows on the wall. Here's one:

> There was once a young boy who grew up in a
> farming village. Every day, he would go out into
> the fields to help his parents. As he grew up, he
> watched the tall glass buildings rise up in the
> distance. And over the years, he watched as more
> and more people came and went between them.
>
> One day, when he was a young man, he entered
> one of those buildings and saw that everyone
> inside was beautiful. They were dressed in tailored

clothing and communicated with their bodies. A
slight lean toward someone made that person very
happy. A handshake between two people made
whole crowds break out in celebration.

The young man wanted to build his own place
where people were beautiful, clothes were tailored,
and bodies spoke happily. But nobody would let
him build on land. So the young man built the
land itself—an island, where even more people
would one day walk through giant glass buildings,
speaking with their bodies and spreading happiness.

Our arms flailed to find balance. I got up
from the mud. My rising shadow was like
that of a rich and powerful leader. I must
have been thirty feet tall.

One of Yang's major influences was Benjamin Franklin. After reading the founding father's autobiography, he remarked, "my takeaway was to do everything with a reason in order to achieve the best outcome. Of one heart, we go!" True to this singularity of purpose, Yang's vision for real estate development in Asia was unprecedented: he was the first to build luxury housing for smaller towns and suburban regions. Forest City in Johor, Malaysia has been the greatest expression of this vision to date.

Yang plans to develop Vietnam next. "Oh comrades! A good company should be welcomed by the world," he often says.

My orthodontist, Dr. Tinloy, had an office across the street from Dr. Don's on Van Ness. The glory of the American Dream could be traced along that famous street, starting from its southernmost tip. There, you could find many of San Francisco's iconic cultural institutions: Davis Symphony Hall, the Asian Art Museum, and the Main Library. Moving north, the Civic Center gave way to UC Hastings College of Law campus, followed by clothing boutiques, movie theaters, car dealerships, steak houses, and office buildings, until, finally, you reached the Russian Hill neighborhood—one of the wealthiest areas of San Francisco, full of Victorian townhouses with views of the Golden Gate Bridge.

Insurance wouldn't cover the cost of the braces. After seeing the bill, my dad looked up at Dr. Tinloy and asked, "Is this necessary?"

"It's entirely cosmetic," the doctor replied. My dad hesitated, then nodded and took out his credit card. A week later, I got my braces.

The appointment took two hours. First, they cleaned my teeth. Then, they covered them with a glue that smelled awful, like nail polish. Next, a number of metal squares were secured to the adhesive. My molars were fitted with hooked metal frames that encircled each tooth like a corset.

Braces feature this particular, tiled configuration because the technology depends on an interaction between a wire strung across your teeth and your teeth's movements. The wire is fed through all the metal mechanisms and then secured to the hooks on the back molars with rubber bands. If some teeth need to be pushed apart, springs are beaded onto the wire, putting pressure on the metal squares in order to push the teeth apart over the course of a few weeks. To pull teeth closer together, rubber bands are attached to the hooked metal frames.

There were two treatment plans for someone with my birth defect. One path was to close the spaces created by the absence of the lateral incisors. The canines would sit next to the front teeth and be reshaped to blend into the smile—to an observer, it might look like something was missing, but it would be hard to figure out

exactly what. The other path was to push
the canines away from the front teeth
to create space for prosthetic incisors.
Anyone with any foresight (my dentist, my
orthodontist, my parents) could see that
a path leading to permanent prosthetics
would be more time-consuming and expo-
nentially more costly. My protocol would
be the first one—to close up the gaps.

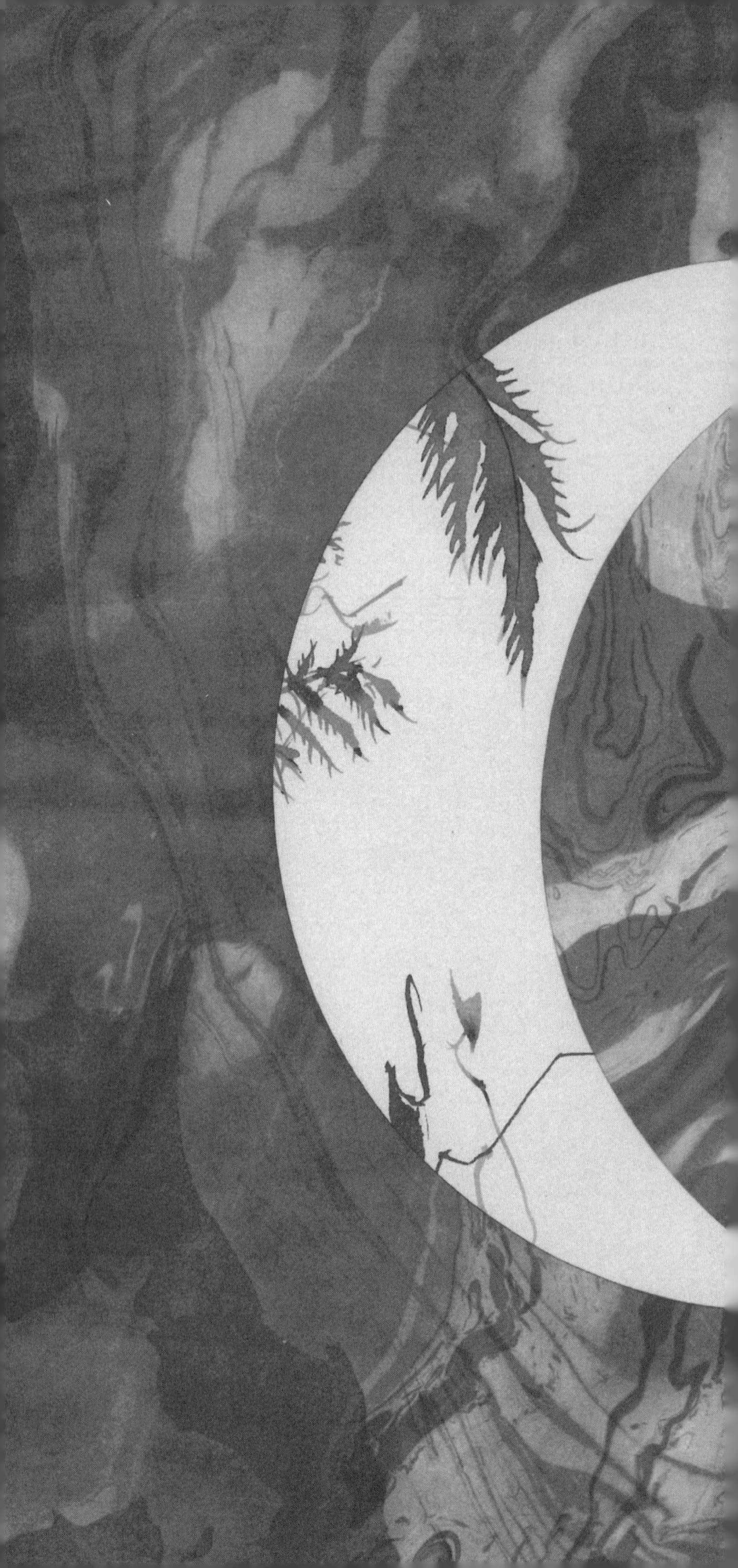

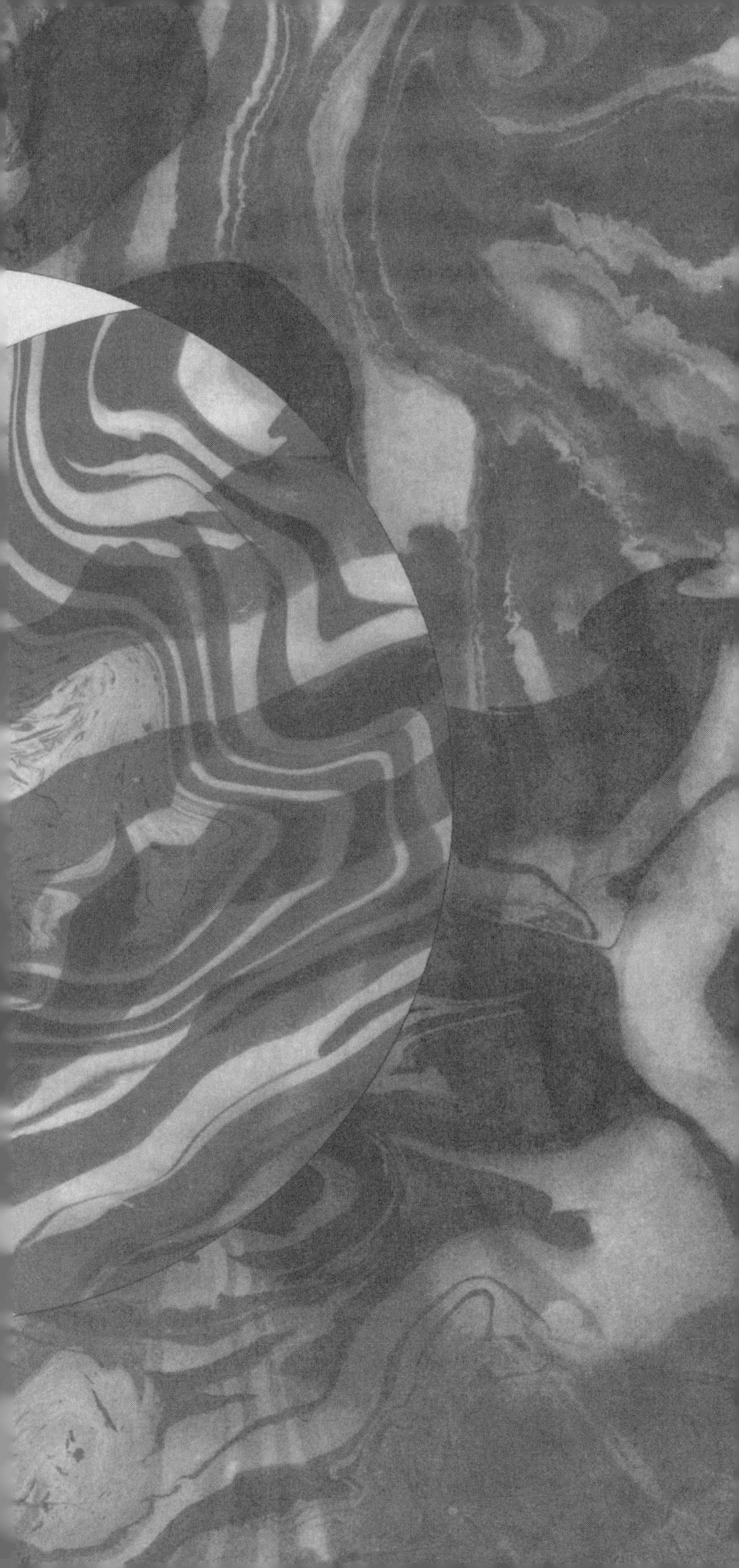

The day after I got my braces was exciting
and painful. I couldn't eat anything, not
even the recommended treat: ice cream.
I remember that phở noodles were the
easiest thing to eat, especially when they'd
been soaked in my mother's broth; if I cut
them up, I could slurp them straight into
my throat and bypass chewing altogether.
By the third week, I was back to normal.
The metal on my teeth had become part
of my body. My lips couldn't remember
a time when the surface of my teeth was
smooth. By then, I was also back to doing
all the things you weren't supposed to do,
like eating popcorn and chewing gum.

On my first routine visit to the
orthodontist, though, Dr. Tinloy made
a consequential decision in a matter of
seconds. He noticed that if my teeth were
to continue moving along the trajectory
they'd started, I would eventually lose
my ability to bite. Without explaining
to me why, he changed my protocol. So
much for the easy and economical path.
The rubber bands came out, the springs
came in; Dr. Tinloy, reversing course, now
started using the braces to push my teeth
apart. One sixteenth of an inch, then

an eighth, then three sixteenths, then a quarter, and on and on: over the next five years, Dr. Tinloy pushed my canines away from my two front teeth using a series of springs. The largest were half an inch long. Throughout middle school and into the eleventh grade, springs became my smile's signature feature.

Missing front teeth makes you worse than ugly. To David Van and my parents, it meant that you were poor and uneducated, and because they believed it, I believed it too. I'm not sure if anyone noticed that two giant openings were being created in my mouth, but I know I found solace in my "mouth full of metal." It kept me from being the girl missing two front teeth.

In my five years of having braces, no one mentioned looks. No one talked to me about beauty. Instead, they talked to me about my bite. The stated goal of any orthodontic treatment is to create or maintain a "good bite"—a bite in which your upper teeth and lower teeth line up correctly, "as nature intended." In a proper bite, the front teeth overlap slightly, and bottom molars act like the

negative mold of the upper; there aren't
any awkward meeting points between your
teeth that would create a risk of grinding.
The other reason people gave for getting
braces was hygienic: less food gets stuck
in a mouth of straight teeth, making them
easier to clean.

But I didn't have crooked teeth. I had
spaced-out teeth; I barely needed to floss.
I didn't grind my teeth either. My bite
was fine.

"Ơ- Ơ- Ơ -Ơ- Ơ- Ơ-Ơ-Ơ."

Trekking through the Phong Nha caves was physically demanding. The area we covered did not always feel the same way on your body as it looked from a distance. The terrain was so angular that our bodies had to mimic the angles of the tipped over, slanted, balanced, and compressed rocks. Using a combination of balance, strength, and guesswork, I learned to move in a triangular fashion, with one foot reaching forward and to the side, onto what appeared to be the next stable rock. Only after I took a step would I often discover that the rock was not just smooth, but silky, causing my whole body to slip. A moment of readjustment: my opposite arm would reach out on a diagonal to steady me, my trailing foot would find another diagonal, my other arm would follow. In this laborious manner, I zigzagged my way through the hollow.

The cave is a vessel of memory. "The Phong Nha Karst is 400 million years old," Đông intoned. "A long time ago, the whole region was water, and you can tell which caves are younger because water still runs through them."

Đông continued to speak as we hiked farther in. "Before tourism, life in Quảng Bình was hard. My village didn't get electricity until 2003. Many people were hunters and gatherers, using hand weapons and oil lamps to gather food and to make a living. You could eat anything you found in the jungle. Most of our meals were wild birds, rats, and small gophers. After many years of hardship and suffering, we have more opportunities now, with more people coming to visit." As he talked, his voice echoed round and round the cave tunnel, his story contouring the hollow cylinder we were passing through.

After we trudged through another underpass, I smelled moisture. I looked up, my headlight probing the cave wall. Soft, graduated watermarks extended horizontally into a glistening surface of blue, black, and brown minerals that faded into white, purple, and gold dust—stains, left by millions of years of water carving out the cavern and defining its contours. As we continued to trek deeper and deeper into the hollow, the light of the sun disappeared behind us. Our headlights became the only sources of light. The group walking ahead of me looked like nervous, frantic guide stars.

Our group descended downward. We hopped off a boulder and onto another landing. Above our heads, spindles of rock hung like dripping candle wax. Tooth-like cones the size of Greek columns started to appear; soon, they were everywhere. They looked like draped Christian statues that had lost their faces. The Virgin Mary's pale double hovered over us. Our headlights animated the cones. It seemed as if the statues were looking at us. I was in church; the cave's hollow seemed to possess a sermon.

We were surrounded by shimmering cave matter: tiny planes of limestone, salt, and gypsum glittered silver and gold. Around us, boulders stacked like ancient books of knowledge. The ground below was a mixture of rock, sand, and shell-like shards. It was as if we were standing on the diseased tongue of a mouth overgrown with teeth.

"Fossil!" one of the porters cried. Buried within the rock was something that looked a bit like a snail, its spiral shell interwoven with the rock's mineral layers. It glistened under our headlights, luminescent white and rust. I could see my breath, glowing in the beam of my headlight. I watched the moisture from my body fog over the buried gastropod.

The silence of our group was interrupted by a group of small black bats that circled around us, unafraid. Their wings made a pleasant whipping sound. Up and down, up and down, they flapped their wings in even angles, mimicking the rocks' triangular geometry. Like a shooting star, a flicker of blue appeared, then another, and another. The swarm of bats became infused with another swarm of blue butterflies. Each butterfly traced a small, even triangle in the air. In an even, frenetic staccato, the butterflies' movements wove into the striding tempo of the revolving bats. From a distance, this blue and black swarm seemed to contour a vessel—a symphonic cyclone, spinning within the larger vessel of this cave we found ourselves within.

Buried in the cave walls were organisms millions of years old, and here before our

eyes was a whirling twister of youth. Bats,
after all, live no more than twenty years,
and many of those butterflies finished
metamorphosis yesterday.

Dr. Don's was not just my dentist's office—it was a Bay Area Vietnamese institution. You entered at 2001 Van Ness, a beautiful San Francisco art deco building with dark green marble and gilded mirrors; the elevator was gold, too. Outside the office door, a sign read "Dr. Nguyên Nguyên, DDS, Dr. Van Nguyễn, DDS, and Dr. Don Nguyễn, DDS." Seldom in America would you see "Nguyễn Nguyễn Nguyễn" engraved on a gold plaque. Dr. Don's father, the original Dr. Nguyễn, was my parents' dentist. Dr. Don's mother, Dr. Nguyễn's wife, was the nurse, receptionist, and operations manager.

My parents socialized with Dr. and Mrs. Nguyễn throughout my childhood. My mother, I remember, was always talking about how fit they were. One year, dressed in the most beautiful clothes, they came to our house a few days before Christmas to drop off a gift. Dr. Nguyễn wore a black tuxedo with micro-blade-thin gold stripes running down his shirt. Mrs. Nguyễn wore and red dress with white pearls in her ears. They were on their way to ballroom dancing. Their confidence

was striking—rare in what I had seen of
Vietnamese people living in America.

Like many Vietnamese refugees, Dr.
Nguyễn had lived a different life in the
mother country. In his youth, he was
part of "Nam Bộ Kháng Chiến," an anti-
colonialist youth movement in Southern
Vietnam. Dr. Nguyễn hung out with
Mai Văn Bộ, who eventually became
a Vietnamese diplomat in Paris, and
Lưu Hữu Phước, a musician and, later,
the cultural minister of the National
Liberation Front. Together, the three of
them wrote the anthem for Southern
Vietnam, "Call to the Youths."

As I kid, I heard Lưu Hữu Phước's
song at least once a year in the Tenderloin,
a small neighborhood on a southern
stretch of Van Ness behind the Civic
Center. Long known for its population of
extremely poor and mentally ill people, it
was also San Francisco's Little Saigon. In
the eight-block area between Geary and
Turk on Larkin Street, you could find the
headquarters of the Vietnamese newspaper
Thằng Mõ, the famous Turtle Tower
Restaurant, and Hiệp Thành Market.

Each year, the Vietnamese community would block off Larkin for an extravagant Lunar New Year Festival where, for several years running, my dad was the master of ceremonies. The festival always included a line-up of Vietnamese musical acts—everything from famous starlets of *Paris By Night* to local dance groups, and maybe a few children's songs from the local Vietnamese school, Âu Cơ. Local restaurants would grill meat, teenagers would light yards of firecrackers, and little kids like me would try to find a few quarters for party poppers.

The cacophonous festival would last all day and into the night. But it always started with a solemn flag ceremony on the center stage. Retired South Vietnamese Army veterans wearing green berets would stand in a line. A few women in *áo dài*, traditional Vietnamese dresses, stood in another. A few would hold South Vietnamese flags, a yellow banner with three horizontal red stripes representing the Northern, Central, and Southern regions of Vietnam. Others would hold the American Flag. A very loud static recording of the anthem would start to

play. "This is Dr. Nguyễn's song!" I would
say quietly to myself, as the crowd began
to sing along:

Oh comrades, let us march to liberation day
Of one heart we go, regret not our living bodies
Together we draw our swords, together we stand up
Until this bitter feud is resolved we will endure

Many years of hardship, how much we've suffered
Gold and silk robbed by the beasts
Their kind, they dig into our blood
Causing miseries, disintegrating families
Mentioning them causes our blood to boil
We vow to destroy those barbarians

Raise our swords, we go to the bitter end
Raise our swords, we vow with our hearts
To the battlefields, fearing not for our lives
Forget not, we're descendants of Lạc Hồng

Oh students, answer to our mountains and rivers
With one heart, go and open the way
Ancient hills and rivers, passed down from our fathers
Brothers and sisters, North and South, we unite

Young spirit like a pure, bright mirror
Regret not your blood; use your talents
Difficult times cannot weaken us
Spikes and thorns, our hearts tremble not
New roads open, seeing far in four directions

Spirit of youth soaring high with bravery
Oh students, go forth under the flag
Oh comrades, unconquerable until now
Go forth with the wind, with all your might
Burning within us a thousand fires

Oh young ones, march on to liberation day
Of one heart we go, regret not our living bodies
The sight of destroyed landscape harden our resolve
The sight of crying people boils our blood with hatred

Risking our lives, eagerly we fight
The flag of justice flutters gold, mixed with blood
Together we march, sweeping the barbarians away
To save our country from dark cycles
In hot blood, we vow to wash away our resentments
Ever after, for our land, praise our heroes

Oh comrades, hurry, march beneath the flag
Oh students, unconquerable until now
Go forth with the wind with all your might
Burning within us a thousand fires

Lưu Hữu Phước—the credited composer of those three young patriots—modeled the melody and structure off of "La Marseillaise," the national anthem of Vietnam's colonizer, France. Bright, positive chords step incrementally into higher pitches, following the brass-led melody. The steady beat of a drum leads them. Despite its many mentions of blood, the sound of the anthem is as clean as a newly forged knife.

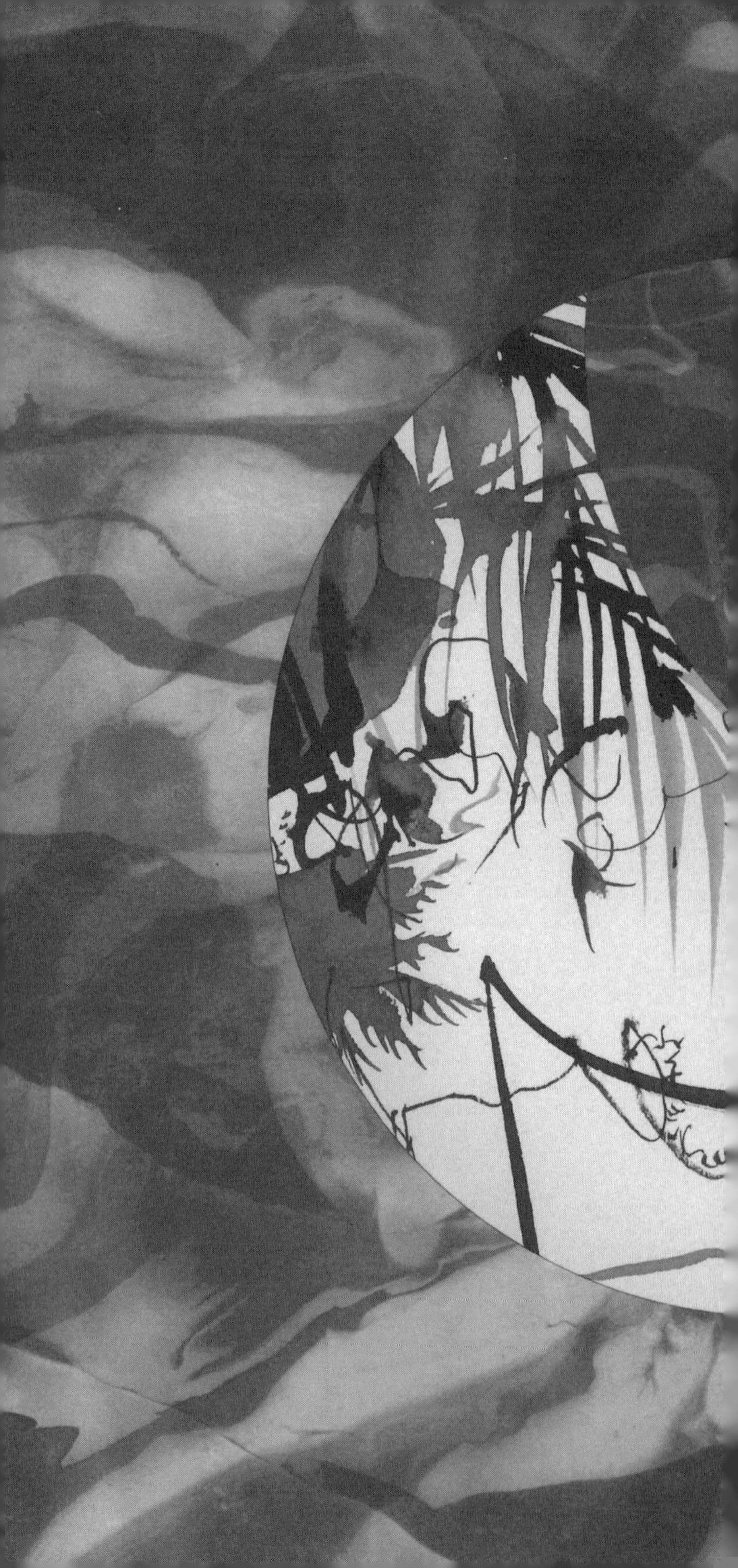

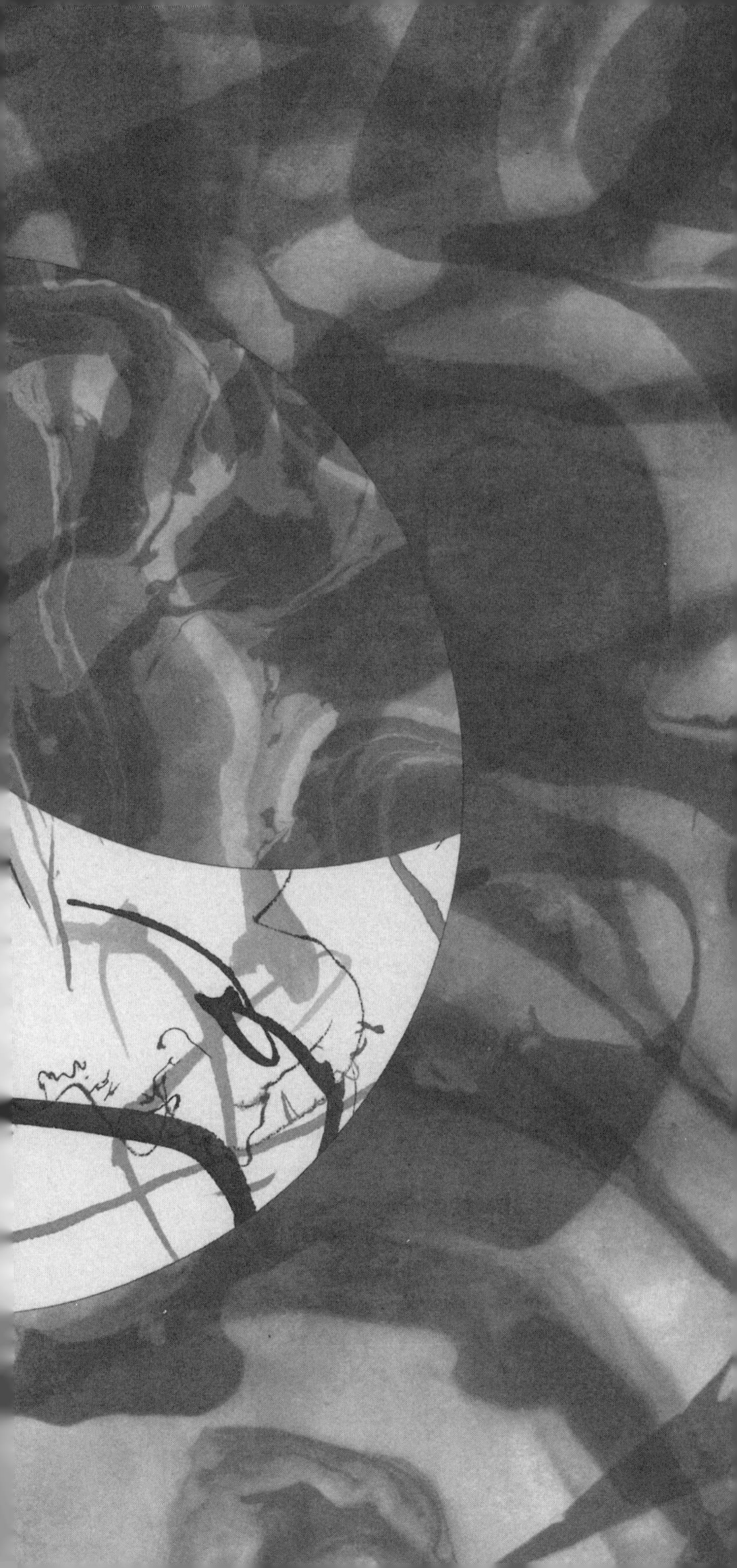

Also known as the Trường Sơn Trail, the Hồ Chí Minh Trail was not a trail in the sense of a path that connects point A to point B. It was a changing, breathing organism: a network of dirt roads, much like the one my group and I were trekking, that started south of Hà Nội in Northern Vietnam and moved southwest into eastern Laos and Cambodia through the Annamite Range, where the Phong Nha Karst lies. Through mountains and jungle, it continued south into eastern Cambodia and terminated in South Vietnam, west of Đà Lạt. Many credit this network, the primary conduit for humans and supplies from North to South, as the reason for North Vietnam's victory in the American War.

Use of the trail began in 1959. The US Navy had blocked the coastline, so the North Vietnamese army needed a new way to transport supplies to the south. Colonel Võ Bẩm of the People's Army of Vietnam, a veteran of the anti-French war of 1946–54, was assigned to the task. Bẩm recalled that, in the anti-French conflict, Việt Minh leaders had created a supply line, the "Reunification Trail," that ran through Vietnam's Central Highlands. He hypothesized that a similar trail, allowing for weapons from the North to be handed off at stations farther south, would give the North and South their best chance at unification.

The soldiers who circuited the trail were called Hà Nội's 559th Transportation Group, and by 1961, there were about 2,000 of them. Their force was amplified by thousands of volunteers—many of them teenagers and women—who kept the network fluid. The heart of this system was the porters, and arguably everyone was a kind of a porter: each person had some kind of a vessel—rucksack, shovel, box, bicycle, truck—that could carry weapons and food to their brothers and sisters in the South.

The United States knew that they needed to eliminate this network in order to win the war, and they tried. They dropped three million tons of explosives—a million more than were dropped on Germany and Japan combined in all of World War II. Chemical defoliants like Agent Orange destroyed thousands of acres of jungle.

But the People's Army of Vietnam had control of the ground; they kept moving. For each crater that the US bombers created, a team of volunteers with shovels filled in the hole. Sometimes they would set traps, tricking the US Air Force into blowing up the side of a mountain so that they could use the gravel that resulted from the explosion.

The trail became the site of daily life for the people who kept the network alive. Songs were sung, pictures were drawn, diaries were written, and plenty of alcohol and smoke were passed around between comrades for the cause. While many Vietnamese died on the trail as a result of bombings, even more succumbed to environmental hazards. Thousands died from heat exhaustion, fever, and snake bites.

The snakes that didn't bite were killed and eaten, along with gophers and other rodents, over salty rice cooked on open fires.

In the summer of 2000, I got my braces off and received my first pair of false teeth. For one week, as I waited for the prosthetic to be made, the gaps in my mouth would be exposed. I was fifteen, and lucky: it was all going to happen while school was on break. No one would see. I hid at home for a week.

I had difficulty speaking, specifically in enunciating "s" sounds. I remember the strange sensation of running my tongue along my bare gums.

On the day of my fitting, the retainer was waiting for me on a silver tray at Dr. Tinloy's office. It was a dainty thing, a transparent pink piece of plastic with two false teeth attached to it by a thin bridge of more pink plastic. When Dr. Tinloy slipped it in my mouth, it didn't look right: there were huge spaces between the prosthetic teeth and my gums. My heart raced. Dr. Tinloy took out the retainer and carved away at the plastic with his dental drill. The adjustments were tedious, but after ten or fifteen rounds of carving, re-inserting, and repeating, something sort of worked. The retainer fit, and the teeth looked acceptable.

As I left with my dad, Dr. Tinloy cautioned, "I wouldn't eat with that thing in your mouth! The teeth are much too fragile." I knew already that I wouldn't follow that rule. What was I going to do, announce to the world that I was missing my front teeth every time I ate?

That day, we went to Great America and rode Top Gun, the rollercoaster where you would fly like an eagle, soaring across the sky as if you were in the US Air Force. David Van had recently convinced my mother that thrill-seeking entertainment was good for one's blood pressure, that it served to "shake things up" and "even everything out" and, for a time, riding the roller coasters at Great America became a bi-weekly excursion, "for the sake of our health."

When I had braces, the wind ran through the gaps of my teeth like big swooshes of ice. But that day, with my new prosthetics, I was so terrified my fake teeth would fly out of my mouth that I clenched my jaw the whole time, waiting for the ride to end. The fear of losing my teeth would follow me for the next nineteen years of my life.

All that I feared happened. Once, my mom accidentally threw out my false teeth while I was brushing my real teeth. Another time, I bit on a straw and the right tooth broke off; I held it together with a piece of chewing gum and ran from school all the way to the dentist's. Another time, I walked into Dr. Don's office for a checkup and told him, embarrassed, that I needed him to look at my prosthetic because I was holding it together with super glue. He ended up snipping off a piece of a paper clip and placing it inside of a hole he dug out of my retainer. Later, in college, I was on a date eating nachos and both of my false teeth broke off. I ran to a bodega, pretending to buy beers for later, and got superglue, which I used to stick my teeth back to the retainer in the taco-bar bathroom. I don't think many people—if any—knew about my situation, unless I told them.

"Before the British came, people lived in the caves, but they did not go in very far. The Vietnamese people are deeply superstitious, even here in Quảng Bình, which is mostly Catholic. They tell stories about ghosts waiting in the caves to catch you."

As we came out of a narrow passage, the cave opened up into a dome. There was a clearing of boulders and sand. The two porters who had been helping us travel created a beautiful spread of the bananas, water, and Oreos they'd carried for us. We ate and drank, doused our faces with water, and took selfies.

Then one porter started to sing. "O-O-O-O-O-O-O-O," The porter's lone voice bellowed around us. He signaled for us to gather our things and continue. "O-O-O-O-O-O-O-O," his singing turned into a familiar wail I had often heard when I was a child. "O-O-O-O-O-O-O-O," cried the porter. I didn't know the song, but his round call stirred deep memories of Vietnamese country songs, like the ones my grandmother would play, loud, from VHS recordings brought over from Vietnam.

The lyrics of these songs often feature the same iconic elements: a bird, a fish, a river, a lover, a longing for a past time. Their melodies are melancholic, each long note slurring into the next with never a bright interval. They almost always end in a fadeout. Wherever I hear these songs—when I would watch *Paris by Night* with my parents and David Van, or today, in any Vietnamese coffee shop with a TV—I can feel the structure of the melody sculpt itself into the physical world. Each word ricochets off whatever surface it can find—a living room couch, a rock, a chair, a leaf—and molds its sadness to the shape of my surroundings.

"These must have been the same songs that were sung in the war," I thought to myself. We were not just walking through geological wonder; these caves were part of the Hồ Chí Minh Trail. I asked Đồng where exactly the trail was.

"It was everywhere," he said, his hands gesturing all around him. "If not for the Hồ Chí Minh Trail, our Brothers and Sisters, North and South, would not have united."

"O-O- O- O -O-O-O-O," Đồng joined the porters' song. "Try to follow my voice, okay? O-O-O-O-O-O-O-O." I could see that we were approaching a narrow passageway. The cave walls tapered above our heads like the ceilings of old gothic cathedrals. We were submerged up to our chests in water, and the path onward was about two feet wide. "Turn off your lights. Just follow my voice," instructed Đông. "O-O-O-O-O-O-O-O!"

Below me, the cave floor continued to protrude: sharp cones, bumpy boulders, round mounds. I braced my hands against the cave walls to help me navigate through the tight waterway. I dragged my legs through the murky cave sediment, brushing across smooth, submerged boulders. My eyes were so wide open, I could feel the muscles around my eye sockets strain. The more I tried to widen my eyes to catch the light, the darker it became.

"O-O-O-O-O-O-O-O," Đông contin-ued to call us forward. As we carried on deeper into the cave, the rocks above and below us seemed to be opening up to water. "O- O-O-O-O-O-O-O," roared the water, the sound coming from a place nearby we could not see.

"Go," said the porter. One by one, we passed through another opening. Though we could not see, we felt the air change. We had entered another hollow, its bowl filled with the water that would carry us into the next region of the karst. One by one, we started to swim, following Đông's guiding call.

One year, David Van and my mom decided that we would all go to Kauai. This was typical; they shared an obsession with health and a fear of dying, coupled with a fixation on wealth, that compelled them to plan frequent excursions "for our health"— always in aspirational, exotic locales. My family did not skimp on accommodations when we traveled. On this trip, we stayed at a Gold Crown resort that was part of a timeshare my parents and David Van owned. The beachfront suite was large enough to sleep all seven of us: my mom, my dad, my sister, David Van, his two kids, and me.

It was a cloudy, muggy day when the Jeep, decked out with *Jurassic Park* decals, pulled up to our resort. We had learned that Kauai was where much of the film had been shot, and we'd booked an action-packed, mountain-road adventure to take us on a tour of the locations. That day, I remember David Van hanging onto one of the Jeep's straps, his eagle tattoo throbbing with his muscles as he laughed. We splashed through pool after pool of mud, and brown water flicked onto our faces and clothes as my cousins and I giggled in delight. Seven hours flew by.

The rest of our vacation was filled with beach play and long drives all over the island to visit new properties. On these vacations, David Van and my parents enjoyed pretending to be real estate investors. They would seek out a local agent and inquire about a new development with such commitment that I wasn't always sure if they were pretending. David Van would drive all seven of us in a rented minivan, sometimes for hours, until we reached a mostly vacant lot of land, the site of some new development that wouldn't be finished for another five to ten years. There was always one model unit that was furnished and decorated as a sales pitch. There was nothing special about the development in Kauai. The walls were white; the unit was air-conditioned; there was a place to grill, a place to park, and a bathtub off of the master bedroom. You had options: studio, one-bedroom, two-bedroom, three-bedroom.

After visiting one of these empty model homes, the agent would take us out to lunch: salad, burger or steak, fruit, maybe ice cream. In the car ride back, my

parents and David Van would debrief, my
uncle taking most of the airtime with his
passionate exclamations. For emphasis,
he might gather his fists and pound them
on the steering wheel. They would run
the numbers on how much you'd need to
rent the unit to make a profit, how much
property taxes were, and, bottom line,
how much better off they were with the
properties they had already bought in the
Bay Area. After the long day, my cousins
and I were always rewarded with more
beach or pool play and a lavish dinner at
an all-you-can-eat buffet, where my dad
never failed to caution me, in front of
everyone, to be careful with my teeth.

This sequence repeated over the next
several years: thrill-seeking entertainment,
real estate tourism, then pool or beach
and an all-you-can-eat buffet. The same
conversations and talking points arose
wherever we were. In Florida, we went
to all of the theme parks of Disney
World and drove all over Orlando
looking for new houses to not buy. In
Vegas, we went through all of the water
amusements and then forayed into the
desert looking for smart investments. In

my years with braces, I only had to be
careful at the buffets. But after I received
my prosthetics, there were times when
I had to take them out at dinner. I was
constantly anxious that my false teeth
would break off in the middle of one of
these vacations, and I would be toothless
in a situation where we needed to look
wealthy and educated.

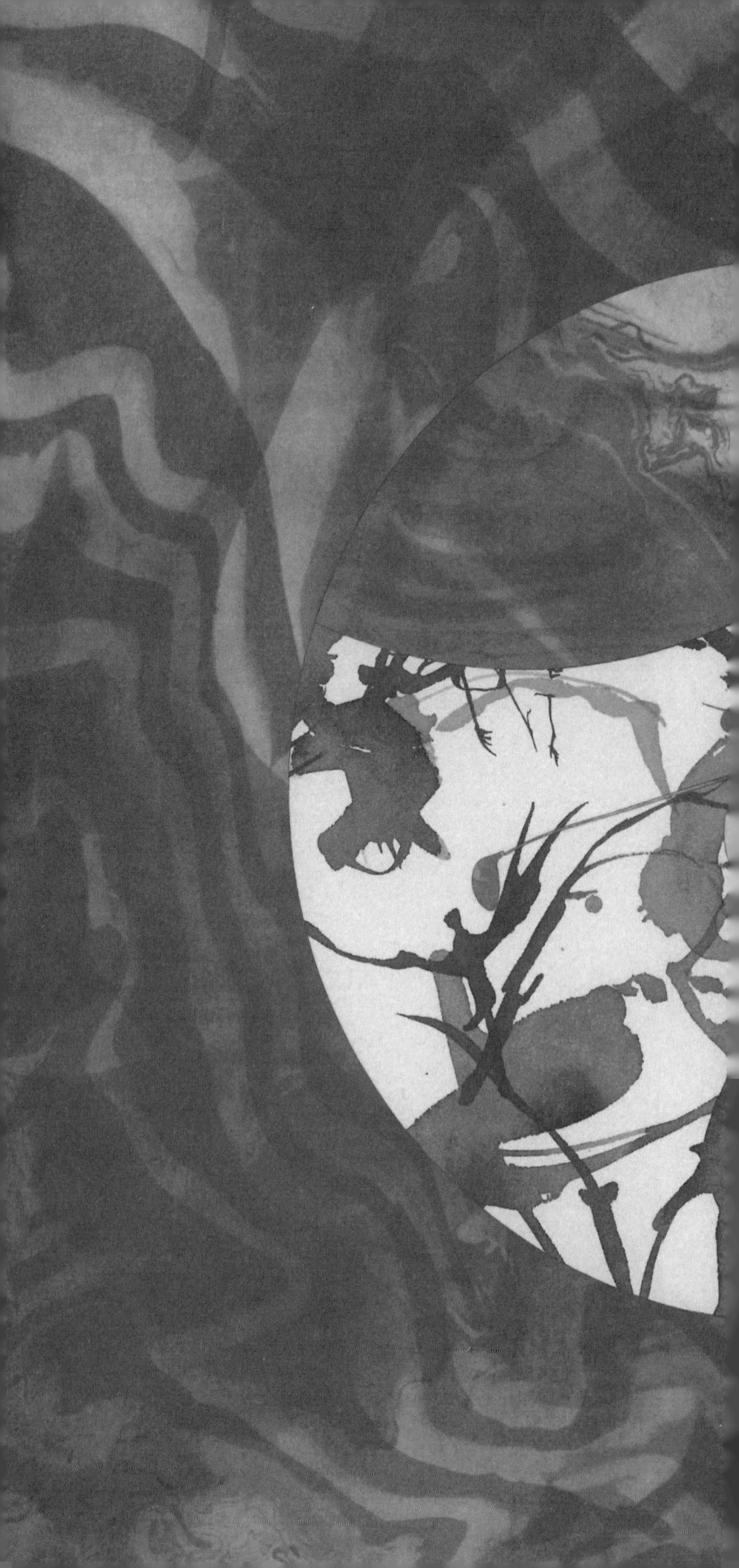

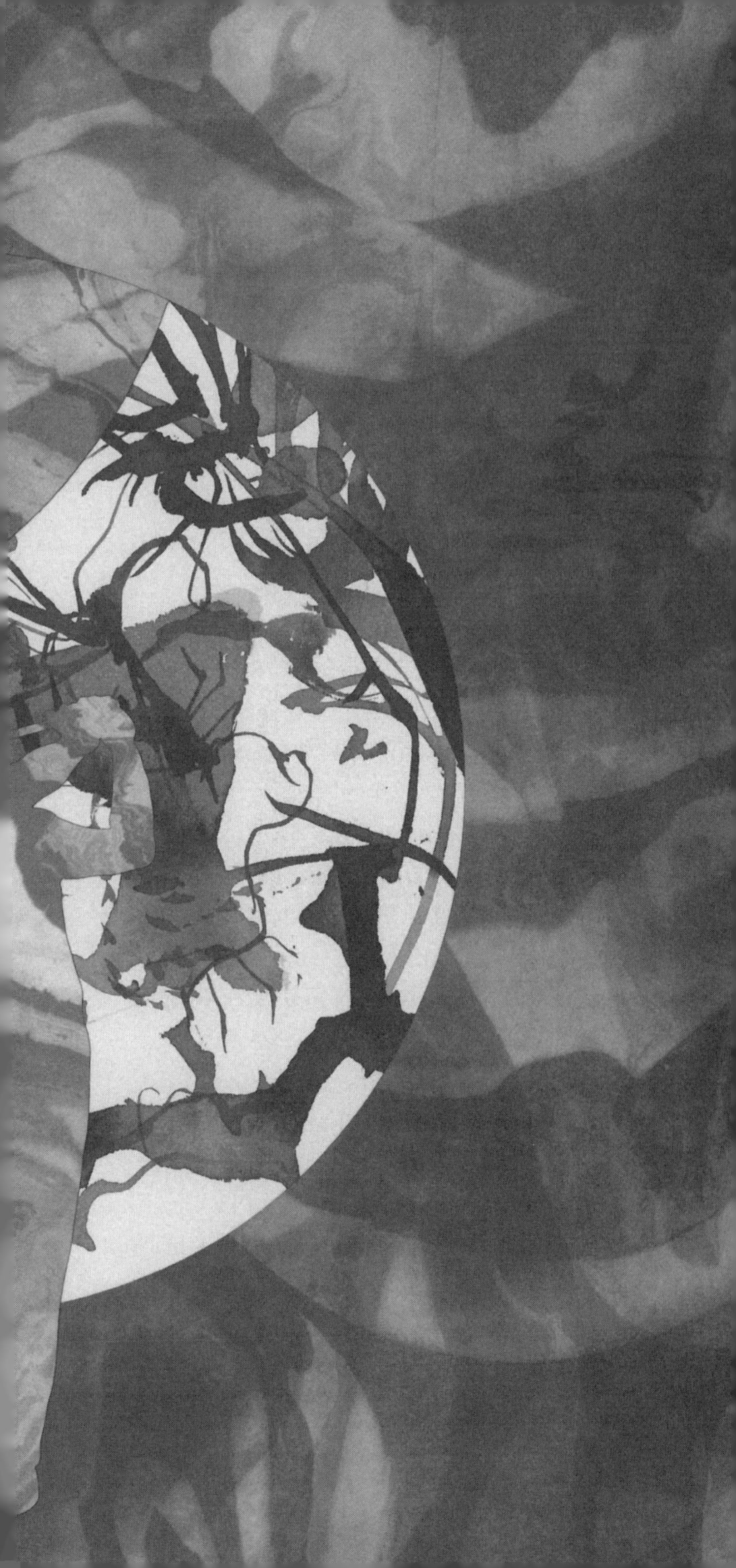

"Ѳ-Ѳ-Ѳ-Ѳ-Ѳ-Ѳ-Ѳ-Ѳ-," I blew bubbles into the cave water through my new front teeth. I was swimming through the darkness of the hollow; my body was completely submerged.

The first sign of light emerged from above as a long, skinny wedge that traced a limestone shard hanging from the cavern ceiling. It was the faintest blue. Then, another long, angular shape appeared, and another, and another. The water, which in the darkness I'd only been able to feel, began to illuminate. Each triangular current of water started to glisten yellow; the entire stream became a tessellation of yellow diamonds reflecting the strengthening light. The surface of the water transformed into a shiny dance floor covered in diamonds flashing as far as my eyes could see. Something about seeing light again felt like salvation.

As we navigated the water, the sun subtly made its presence known. From darkness into palest light, I could see the curves of the cavern again. Around the final corner, the exit showed its bright circle, as if to say "come here." The hole was like a young spirit, a mirror, so pure and bright it hurt. I squinted so the light could rest on my eyelashes until, slowly opening my eyes, I gradually let it in.

"O-O-O -O-O-O-O -O!" As the waterway opened into a wider, river-like path, Đông swam ahead; his call became a country song. Framed by the contours of the cave mouth, Đông was a black shape rimmed with sunbeams, a risen Jesus.

Most things seemed familiar, but I was looking at them a little differently. I noticed that plants grew wherever the sunlight hit the rocks; that the rocks' illuminations were compounded by the glow off the edges and angles of branches and leaves. Whatever the sun touched seemed to be bathing, gleefully, in the good light.

It was easier to balance from rock to rock on the way out. The air was not as thick. The breeze blowing in from the exit, when we could catch it, gave a cooling touch. One white lit surface, then two, then three, then a mosaic of seven: the rocks found dramatic contours against dark grey-blues as we approached the cave's opening. Seeing the sun again was exciting but difficult. The cave mouth was

a giant white screen; I had to look at the
dark spaces around it until, eventually, my
eyes adjusted.

Việt Nam's Constitution of 1992
Article 32

1. *Every one enjoys the right of ownership with regard to his lawful income, savings, housing, chattel, means of production, funds in enterprises, or other economic organizations.*

2. *The right of private ownership and the right of inheritance are protected by the law.*

3. *In cases made absolutely necessary by reason of national defense, security, and the national interest, in case of emergency, and protection against natural calamity, the State can make a forcible purchase of or can requisition pieces of property of individuals or organizations against compensation, taking into account current market prices.*

"It is impossible to count the number of species of plants in Phong Nha," Đông told the group as we emerged from the cave and pried our way through the jungle. Each corner of my vision was oozing with life, but a kind of life that wasn't nice, welcoming, or virtuous. Here, the jungle fluttered with a density of leaves in tiny, small, large, and enormous sizes. Spikes and thorns twisted around like the crown of Christ. The frond of a palm stuck out, a raised sword—though you could not see who had drawn the weapon. Vines twirled around like venomous snakes. Another branch with an abundance of tongue-shaped leaves lapped water. Long grasses stuck out from every dark crevice like patches of dry hair. Star fruits hung from above like sleeping bats, and tamarind pods hung from other branches, pregnant with seeds. The jungle lured you with its beauty, flirting with your fascination. While some plants were medicinal and many could be eaten, there were others that could make you itch and some that could kill you. It was a morality-free terrain.

When I looked back to the cave's opening, it looked like the sun: a big round disc hitting the cave rock with its bright good light. The sun kissed our wet faces and we could smell food roasting on hot coals. At the next clearing, we were greeted with a wholesome spread of tropical fruit and sweet biscuits. The porters were there already, cooking for us; clay pots of rice and jugs of tea were brought out as we gathered around.

"Did the early cave dwellers ever make pots out of the mud from the cave?" I asked.

"Yes!" Đồng said excitedly. "In fact, you can sometimes see their ceramic remains in the rocks. You can tell that people really lived there."

A porter brought out a vessel of herbs. It was time to eat.

My husband and I sat with the Dutch dentist couple. Our lunch was grilled pork and omelettes wrapped with rice crepes and dressed with an assortment of herbs and *cheo,* known as "jungle sauce," a dipping concoction unique to the Quảng Bình region. The flavor of the cheo was delicious and overwhelming; it framed the common flavors of the rest of the ingredients and made them belong to this place. Taste sensations floated around my mouth and around my new implants, exciting the nerves along my gums.

"How long have you guys been dentists?" I asked the Dutch couple.

"Well, actually, I'm a dentist, but he is in school for oral surgery," the woman said.

"Oh wow, I just got implants!" I was excited.

"Oh really? Which ones?" the man asked.

"My lateral incisors."

The two of them smiled in acknow-ledgment.

"Very common, very common," they both nodded.

"They look great," the woman said.

"Thank you," I replied.

"It is very expensive to do that in America, no?" the woman asked.

My husband and I both laughed, nodding our heads yes.

"And it took forever," I said. "How much is it for one in the Netherlands?"

"So little, so little compared to America, maybe 700 US dollars," said the man. "But nothing is as good as in America."

The woman laughed in agreement. "America has the best dental technology. Nothing beats the American smile."

In 2007, 22 years old and a recent college grad, I moved to Sài Gòn. In my mouth was my fourth pair of prosthetic teeth.

David Van would call me every so often, just to say hello, and I enjoyed talking to him as I drove around the fast-developing city. He would tell me that I reminded him of himself when he was young and running around Sài Gòn. He'd ask if I'd kept up my blog and tell me how much he liked seeing my pictures and reading my stories. There were two things he would ask me to do for him. One was to go to the Citibank to collect the money he'd sent for my grandmother's caretakers. The other was to drive by Saigon Pearl, a new real estate development where he had recently made a big down payment. I did both. I lived in an industrial part of town, and I would drive my motorbike to the center to stop at Citibank, then loop over to Saigon Pearl, and then to my aunt's house to give her the money so she could pass it along.

There was rarely anything to see at Saigon Pearl. The development occupied a long stretch of road, maybe 400 meters, but it was boarded up with a grey-green

aluminum fence on which blue letters
spelled out "Saigon Pearl." Elsewhere,
a billboard displayed renderings of
apartments overlooking the Sài Gòn River.
Somewhere, a slogan declared "Luxury
Saigon." But you could tell that, behind
the fence, there was nothing but a couple
of cranes and a pile of dirt.

Two years later, David Van died suddenly of a heart attack. Everyone was shocked that someone so big, strong, and beautiful could die so abruptly. The police found his rotting corpse alone in his bed after they responded to a complaint about a foul smell secreting from his house.

I was 24 and still living in Sài Gòn. Not long after his death, I was at a business meeting, trying to score a commission for myself and some friends to paint a mural at a cafe that was still under construction. There I was, pitching a wall painting of abstract trees and changing seasons and sipping an iced coffee. There was plenty of small talk and laughter as we chatted about colors: how to make the trees look like a Vietnamese forest, how to make the cafe look expensive. Then I bit on a piece of ice that snapped my right false tooth off. Quietly panicking, trying to maintain a networking-cool facade, I navigated the meeting to a "let's keep talking" conclusion. Before I got on my bike, I called an uncle of mine whose wife was a dentist. Without telling him why, I asked if I could see her right away.

I zipped through the city to get to her office, passing by the Saigon Pearl on the way. Something had changed there. A tall grey tower had been built. It had no windows yet; way up high in the sky, a crane appeared to be in the process of adding more floors.

Since the fall of Sài Gòn in 1975, over seventy Western films have been made about the Vietnam War. These include classics like Francis Ford Coppola's *Apocalypse Now* and Oliver Stone's *Platoon, Pinkville,* and *Heaven & Earth.* None of them were shot in Vietnam. As Jenni Trang Lê, a Vietnamese film producer, would later explain to me, Vietnamese censorship prevented most films from shooting in this most "unreal" of places.

"Nothing that makes the government look bad. Nothing that makes the country look bad. Nothing that is too sexy. Nothing that is too scary. Nothing that is too violent. Oh, and no zombies."

"No zombies?" I asked.

"No zombies—not if the zombies are made in Vietnam. If it's a zombie movie made in Korea or America, that's okay. Korea and America can have zombies. They just don't want people thinking that Vietnam has zombies."

I had been a patient of Dr. Neal Fujishige for a few years when I told him that I finally wanted to undergo the procedure. I asked for a cost estimate; I knew that permanent implants would be expensive, and insurance was unlikely to cover much, if any, of the cost, because it is considered cosmetic surgery. The estimate came back: $15,000. I swallowed air, thought of David Van and the American smile, and said I wanted to proceed.

Think of an implant like a screw in a wall. The longer the screw, the more secure it will be and the more weight it can carry. A successful implant needs at least ten millimeters of space going up into the gums in order to provide a strong hold. In cases like mine, while the gaps where the lateral incisors should be appear large, there usually isn't enough room between the bones of the front teeth and those of the canines for an implant to fit. The precision of the angle is also extremely important, because the area is close to the sinuses—parts of the respiratory system connected to the nose and throat. If the angle of the implant is off, permanent nerve damage could result.

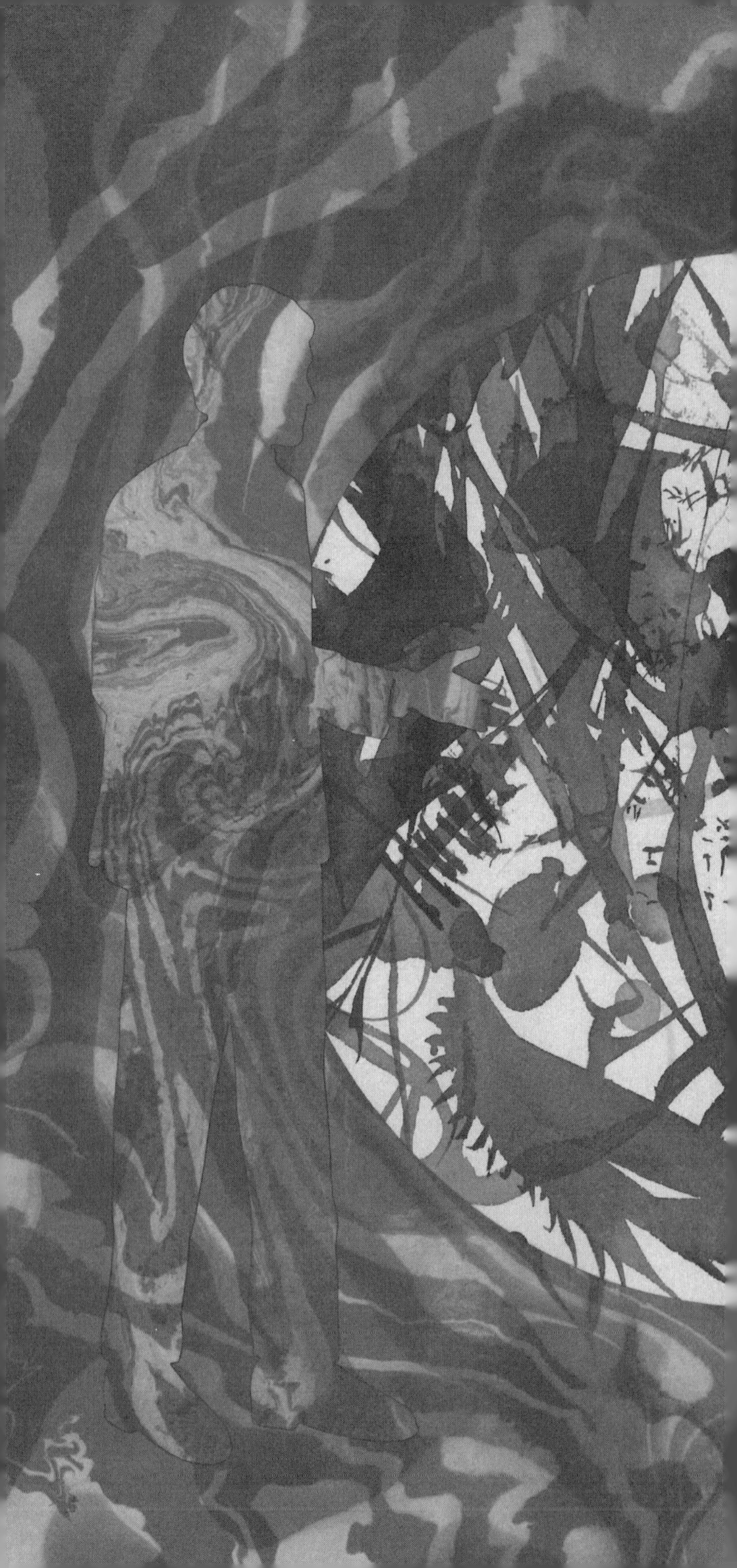

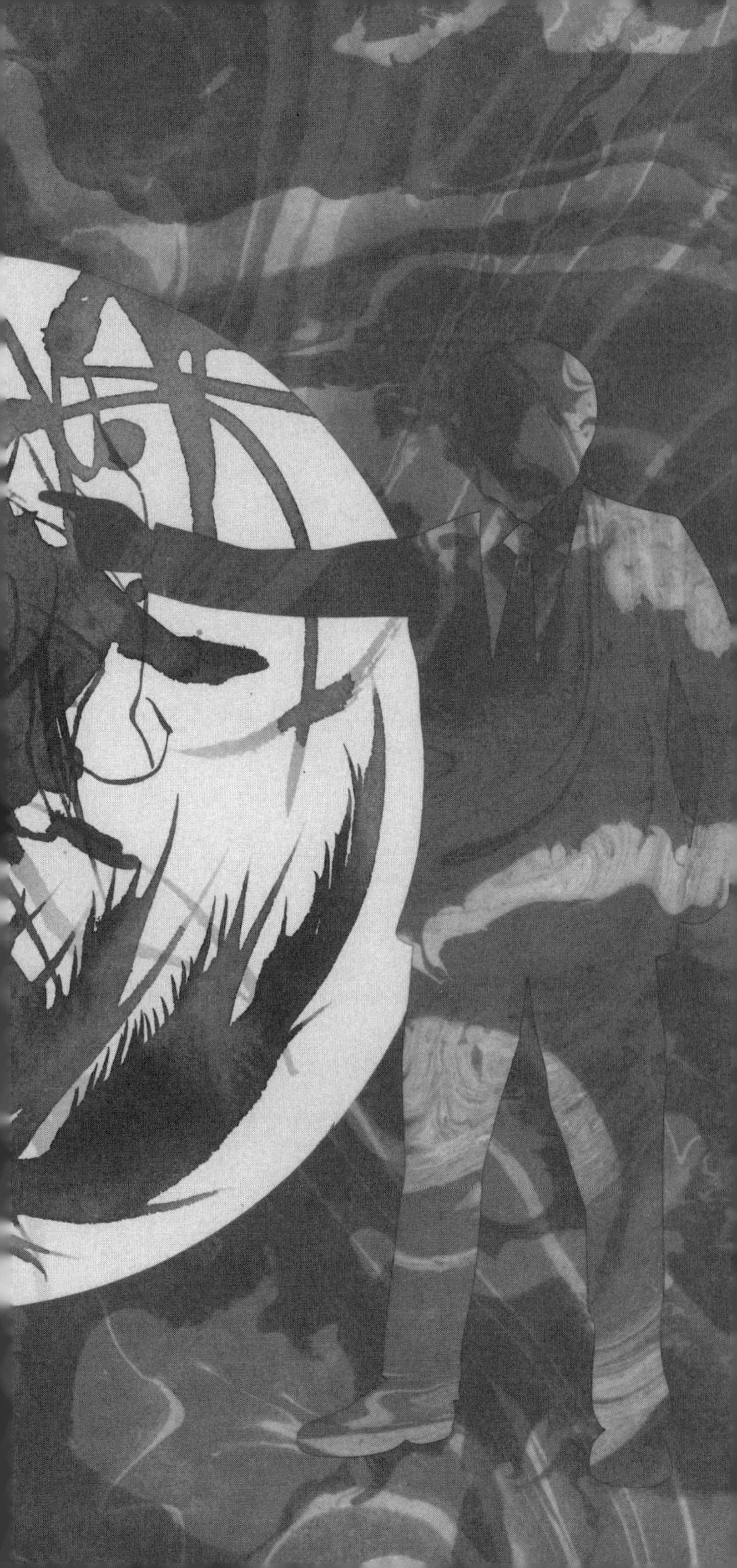

Dr. Fujishige was concerned about aesthetics: "It needs to be perfect, it needs to be perfect," he told me again and again. Since the lateral incisors are so visible, Dr. Fujishige was adamant that they look seamless—as if I were born with them.

To prepare my mouth to receive the implants, I was prescribed six months of Invisalign—another $5,500. Dr. Fujishige's goal was to get the bones of my front teeth and canines to move as far away from each other as possible before we made the attempt. My concern, as always, was to not let anyone see that I was missing teeth.

The fitted, clear-plastic Invisalign molds required another level of creative eating. I had gotten used to my prosthetics—I'd been wearing them for eighteen years. I knew how to bite a carrot using only my front teeth. I would cut steak into pieces small enough to use only my molars to chew. I never bit into whole apples. Aligners were different—most people take them off during meals. But for me, that would mean excusing myself to a bathroom, removing them without letting my fake teeth fall into the toilet, and re-inserting my prosthetic—then reversing the steps twenty minutes later, once lunch was over.

After two months and four aligners, Dr. Fujishige was disappointed in the lack of bone movement. He adjusted the procedure, giving me a whole new set of aligners, this time with "attachments." In aligner-speak, attachments are tooth-colored pieces of plastic that are fused to the surfaces of your teeth to provide additional traction as the aligners pull your bones into their new shape. Now, my front teeth and canines all had plastic fused to them. It was almost like having braces again.

I flew to Johor, Malaysia from Hồ Chí Minh City on the morning of August 4, 2019 to visit Forest City. As the airplane made its descent, I could make out a shoreline of flat, sandy land with grey developments sprouting from the plain. Miles away, I saw the sprawl of Johor's untouched jungle.

Forest City is a man-made island located in the Johor Strait, two kilometers away from Singapore and another two kilometers from mainland Malaysia. Its construction began in 2015. Its developer Country Garden partnered with Sultan Ibrahim of Johor for the project. Forest City has been called a "present-day Atlantis"; it claims to be the world's foremost sustainable city. It runs solely on renewable energy and is able to reabsorb 10,000 tons of carbon from the air each year. When Forest City is completed, it will be covered in greenery: nearly one million plants, made up of more than 100 species and 40,000 individual trees. This utopia on the water is also completely tax free.

Forest City was about thirty minutes by car away from the Johor International

Airport. Mr. Aw picked me up in a silver Toyota. He was a soft-spoken but efficient man; he didn't waste any time explaining my itinerary. I was being taken to a welcome lunch; I would then tour all of the properties, concluding with the resort next to the new golf course where the developer had gifted me a one-night stay in the King Suite.

I had been in conversation with Mr. Aw for a year, ever since I contacted Forest City's sales office and told them I was a professor and artist in New York City with frequent business in Asia. Texting Mr. Aw on WhatsApp, I shared with him that I would be exhibiting my paintings in Hồ Chi Mính City in August of 2019 and would like to visit Forest City to explore the prospect of purchasing an investment property. Over the months leading up to my arrival, Mr. Aw sent me copious amounts of well-designed informational material about Forest City— as well as Christmas, New Year, and Lunar New Year greetings. And now, there I was: a prospective buyer dressed in black.

The highway in Johor was clean and lined with trees. After a large onramp, Forest City rose from the horizon. A giant billboard covered in shrubbery read, "FOREST CITY." A collection of identical white towers grew higher and higher as we drove closer. To my right-hand side, a big complex that looked like a convention center appeared, with impressive metal lettering across its roof: "SHATTUCK-ST. MARY'S FOREST CITY INTERNATIONAL SCHOOL." Not many cars were going our way, but the ghostly city shimmered with excitement. A security booth greeted us upon arrival. As the guards inspected his ID, Mr. Aw smiled at me and said, "They always want to know who is here because everything is tax free. First lunch, okay?" I nodded.

We parked in an underground lot and took an elevator up to what looked like a high-tech contemporary mall. Well-lit, air-conditioned, glass windows from floor to ceiling, white marble floors, zigzagging escalators leading to glistening landings. And fake plants everywhere: these splayed over the balconies and erupted in potted arrangements every few feet. There was even a string of plastic leaves wrapped around the cord of the hand-drying machine in the bathroom.

The dining area was vast and dim. The buffet itself was spotlit, an oval stage for a performance starring international cuisine: giant prawns drenched in a coconut peanut sauce, sautéed cabbage, pasta with multiple sauces, curry stewed chicken, stir-fried beef, rice, a variety of pickled vegetables, and a fountain of Sprite. There was hardly anyone there, just a trio of chatty Hanoian women and a young Chinese family in a far, lonely corner. I had a little of everything, and so did Mr. Aw. He told me how, unlike Vietnam, everything in Forest City is clean; that it's a great place for kids; that, because all the cars are underground, there's no pollution above. Great schools, in case my kids want to get into Harvard. And a wonderful place for old people because of Malaysia's mild tropical climate.

After lunch, we ascended an escalator to the second floor, where we were greeted by a giant vinyl poster of a man wearing a cowboy hat. "That's Mr. Yang Guoqiang, founder of Country Garden," Mr. Aw informed me. Right as we got off, we came to an enormous scale model of Forest City. The floors of different complexes blinked in an alternating pattern to give the appearance of a bustling paradise. Restaurants were lit with blue and magenta LEDs; boats and yachts were glued to an ultra-blue resin pour standing in for the water. Giant signs read "Commercial Street" and "Transportation Hub." We were greeted by another man, a sales representative for the Forest City luxury apartments. A jovial man with a "smiling with your eyes" face.

The Smiling Salesman ushered me through a door, and I found myself in a black box theater. It was enormous; the walls were made out of speakers and the screen wrapped around half of the room. Once I was seated, the lights dimmed dramatically. It quickly became dark.

"𝒪- 𝒪- 𝒪 -𝒪- 𝒪- 𝒪-𝒪-𝒪," the film came on with a crescendo of brass instruments you might hear in *Jurassic Park* or *King Kong*. Aerial panoramas of Forest City swish-panned into view, accompanied by the sweeping orchestral adventure-movie score. Following the brass-led melody, bright, positive chords incrementally stepped into higher pitches. Each cut in the film was accompanied by that familiar epic swoosh that you might hear when King Kong leaps from rock to rock. *Swoosh*: King Kong grabs a soldier and flings him into oblivion. *Swoosh*: businessmen stalk the giant glass halls of Forest City, wielding briefcases, making decisions, lecturing in high-tech conference rooms.

A man speaking in the gravelly American accent of every blockbuster trailer narrates over the spectacle:

> *It is an economic inspiration. The Association of Southeast Asian Nations boasts prime location and solid foundation for economic and trade cooperation and is becoming a growth engine for Asia's economic development. Malaysia is one of the fastest-growing counties in Southeast Asia, the most attractive investment destination in the world. FOREST CITY, adjacent to Singapore, is located in Iskandar Development Region, the development corridor of southern Johor, Malaysia. It lies in the south of Malacca Straits leading to various APEC Countries, connected to the Trans-Asian Railway.*

Swoosh: Freight ships sailed across the deep blue sea.

Swoosh: A crane lifts a giant container onto shore.

Swoosh: A man dressed in a suit looks up at the sun in the sky and smiles.

FOREST CITY combines cutting-edge concepts and technology in smart and eco-city management. It truly reflects COUNTRY GARDEN'S pioneering spirit in creating an industry-integrated green and smart city.

Swoosh: A chef opens a case of live crabs, to the excitement of a group of female socialites.

Swoosh: Two small children run up to their mother, who is reading a book by a clear blue pool.

On January 22, 2016, FOREST CITY's global launch drew worldwide attention. In June and September 2016, the Malaysian government issued two official policy papers to designate FOREST CITY a duty-free area, making it the most favorable economic zone in Malaysia. The Signing Ceremony of the Strategic Initiative of Forest City was held on December 6, 2016. FOREST CITY signed MoU with thirty-six domestic and international enterprises, of which nine were among the WORLD TOP 500.

Swoosh: A man proposes to his girlfriend underneath a coconut tree.

COUNTRY GARDEN FOREST CITY: A Prime Model of Future Cities.

The lights came back on, so pure and bright it hurt. I squinted so the light could rest on my eyelashes until, slowly opening my eyes, I gradually let it in.

The Smiling Salesman appeared on the far side of the room, showing me through another door.

"When can we get moving on this?" I asked Dr. Fujishige.

Dr. Fujishige wanted me to have the best surgeon in New York City, someone who would be as meticulous as he was. After an unsuccessful phone consultation with a Canadian in Midtown Manhattan, he forwarded me to Dr. Harrison Chen, another Midtown oral surgeon. Dr. Chen could not have been more than 40 years old. He was very kind, with an extremely strong handshake that reminded me of David Van. He was fit, built like some of the porters in Phong Nha. His confidence was intimidating. Our consultation took about 30 minutes: twenty minutes in the waiting room and ten, at most, with him.

After he shook my hand, he took a quick glance at the screen, then turned to me. "Say O-O-O-O-O-O-O-O." Dr. Chen poked his circular mirror around in my mouth. In another mirror that I had been given to hold, I watched him probe my upper gums.

"I can do this. I can work with this," he confirmed.

"That's it?" I asked. "Why has everyone, my entire life, made such a big deal out of this surgery?"

"Everyone is different. But I can do this."

"What about swelling? I need to know how much swelling."

"Not much."

"Will my prosthetic fit, after?"

"Easy."

A week later, after Dr. Fujishige had given it the green light, the operation was booked for July 12, 2018.

"No climate change here," the Smiling Salesman said as I entered the showroom.

Behind a wall covered in plastic plants was an enormous diorama which diagrammed the history and vision of Forest City. A label read "STRATEGIC LOCATION." Below it, a giant green plexiglass map of the world showed Forest City's centrality to a whole network of countries and cities, with thin blue lines uniting them under the One Belt, One Road vision: Singapore, Malaysia, Indonesia, Brunei, Philippines, Haikou, Sanzhou, Xi'an, Lanzhou, Urumqi, Khorgas, Kazakhstan, Kyrgyzstan, Tajikistan, Uzbekistan, Iran, Sri Lanka, India, Turkey, Russia, Kenya, Greece, Italy, Germany, Holland. Beneath that, five green illuminated discs read: Tropical climate, 21°C–32°C, PM 2.5 = excellent, UV index = comfortable 5–8.

The Smiling Salesman gestured at another model, a big cross-section of the man-made land mass with a blinking line indicating the different stages of the process. Lots of places have been made from reclaimed land, he said, like Palm Islands in Dubai and Changi Airport in

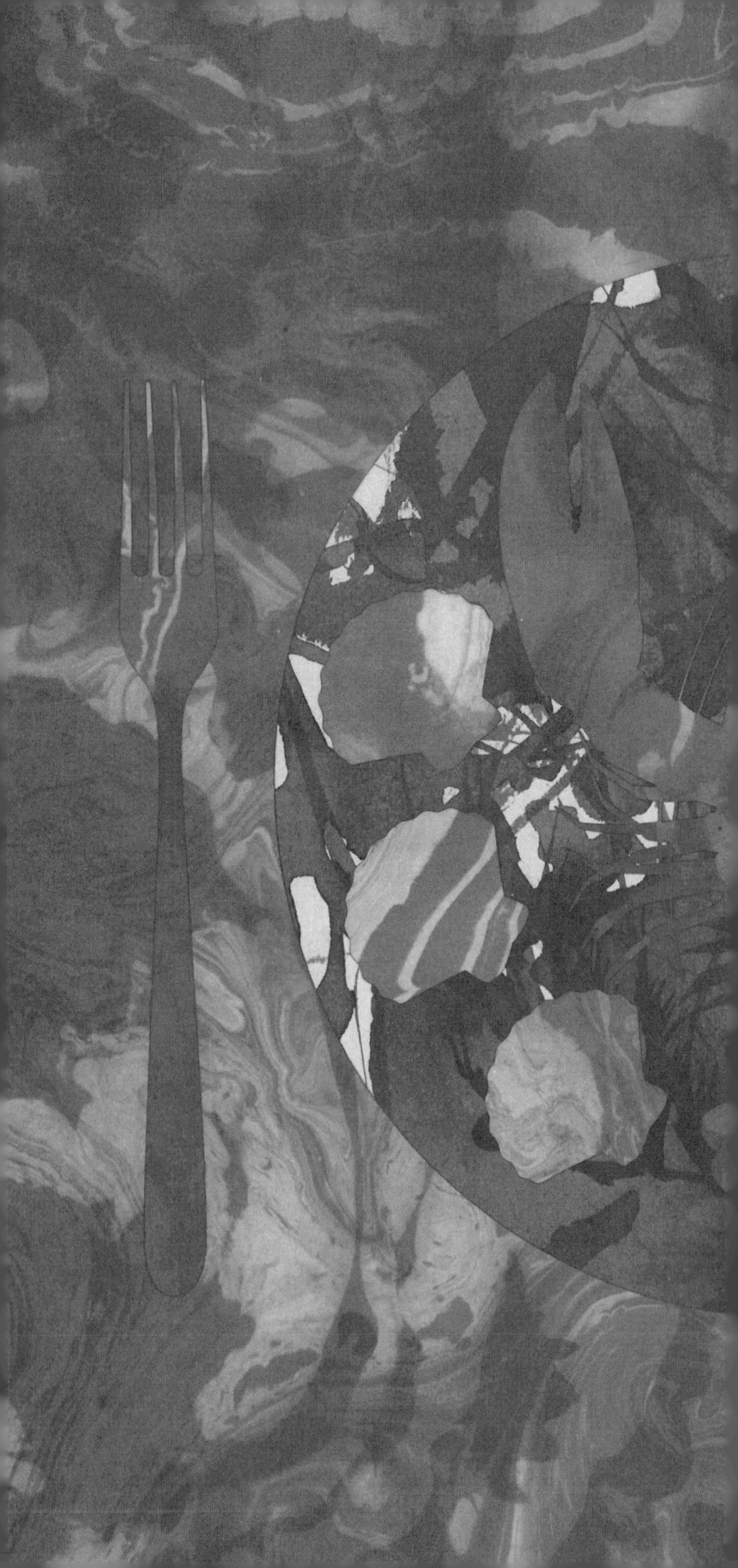

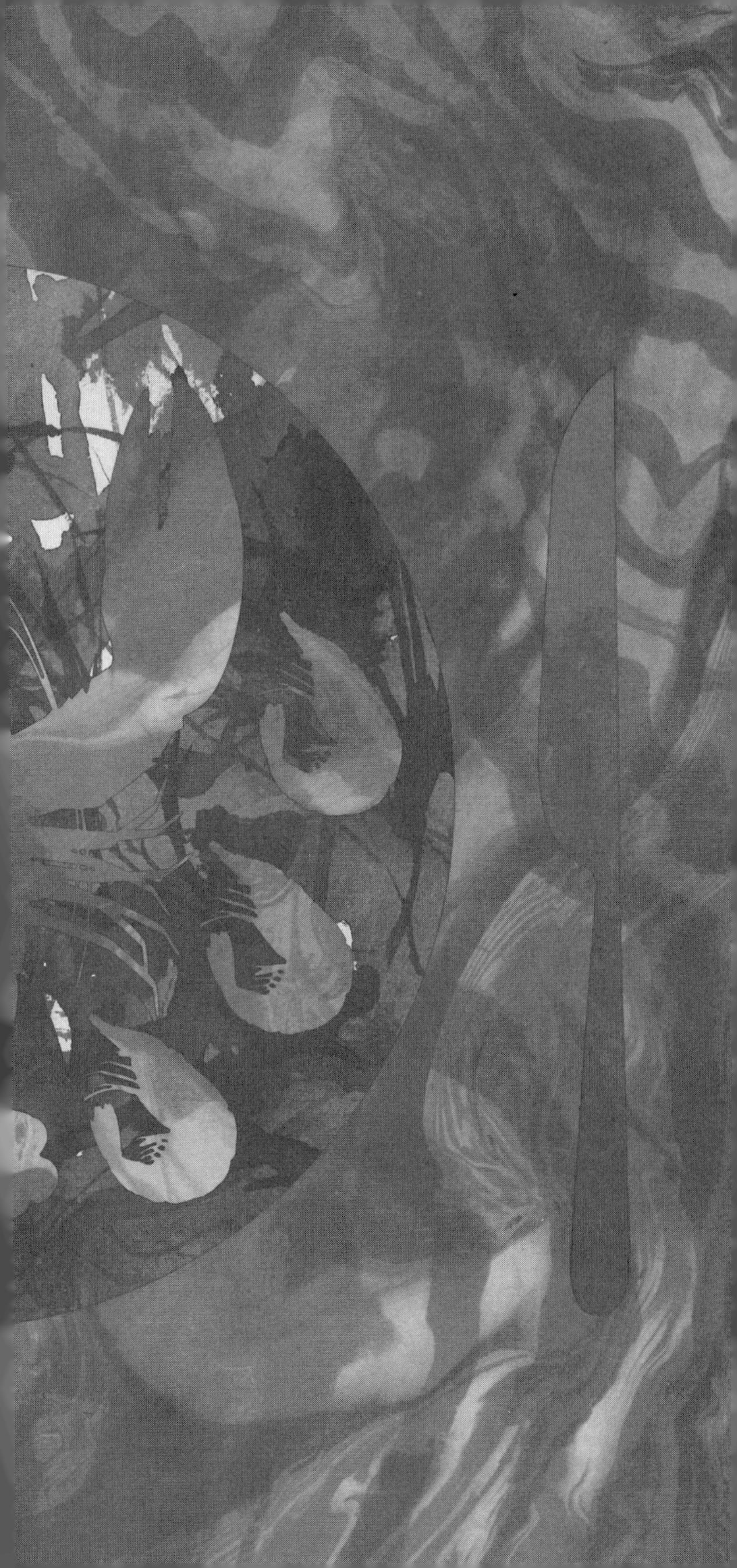

Singapore. "Reclaimed land technology is very advanced," he said, pointing to the three layers of earth in the model: rock, soil, sand. "The rock and soil are found onsite, but the sand is brought in from elsewhere to create the land mass, hence the term 'reclaimed land.' You can only create reclaimed land where the sea is not very deep. Here in Forest City, the sea is just two to six meters deep. It's been built to its maximum size."

As the Smiling Salesman told me this, I thought about what I'd been reading about the cost of this imported sand. Small islands not far from Forest City, in the Riau Islands of Indonesia, had disappeared overnight. Their sand was loaded onto ships which sailed off into Singaporean waters, just 20 minutes away by commuter ferry.

After the land is compressed, concrete and steel pipes are drilled thirty to forty meters deep through the sand, soil, and rock. This process, called "piling," gives the man-made land the necessary strength to support the weight of the island's buildings, cars, and people: its society. All of the buildings that make up Forest City were designed and manufactured at the industrial park within the nearby special economic zone. After the land was ready, the parts were driven over the bridge and assembled with cranes.

Below the land-building model was a quote that read:

> *With blue skies, white clouds, pure sea breeze and haze-free air all year round, it is the most livable country in Asia.*

The Smiling Salesman took me to another wall with a giant map of the Iskandar Special Economic Zone. Guided by his laser pointer, I learned that the Zone exists because of Singapore; that Singapore is a small country—only 719 square meters, and 30% of it is reclaimed land, including its airport and its recreational island, Sentosa; that, even though Singapore is smaller than Hong Kong, it's doing pretty well; and that, because Singapore can't get any bigger, in 2006, Malaysia saw an opportunity to claim some of Singapore's business growth.

The Smiling Salesman's laser pointer circled, focusing in on the different zones of Iskandar. Zone E holds the Johor

International Airport; Zone A is the old city center where the first bridge to Singapore was built, but it was outdated, and poorly planned in the first place; Zone B is considered the new city center. The island of Forest City lies to the south of the entire zone.

There are seven universities here, the Smiling Salesman went on, and all are ranked in the top 200 globally. He told me that education used to be better in Singapore, and Malaysia used to have no schools, but now some of the British universities have opened campuses there— including the Marlborough School's Asian campus, where Kate Middleton studied. Since these institutions relocated, many Singaporeans have started to settle in Malaysia.

Zone B is also a cultural zone, I learned. Malaysia is proud to have the first Lego Land in Asia, as well as the new Pinewood Iskandar Malaysia studios, a Hollywood film studio that is already turning a profit. Zone B is also where the hospitals are located. Because everything in Malaysia is about 60% cheaper than in Singapore, more and more people are coming to take care of their medical needs. The Gleneagles Medini Hospital has the ability to do anything that the one in Singapore can do, but cheaper.

The Smiling Salesman looked at me and said, "For the price of one property in Singapore, you can buy seven in Forest City. And there is no tax here and it's FREEHOLD. In Singapore, you can only have a 99-year lease on your property. It is FREEHOLD in Malaysia."

The Smiling Salesman's laser pointer circled one cluster of apartments, then another. "Those apartments are Phase 1, and those are Phase 2. They're sold out." He pointed to a third cluster. "Those are Phase 3, and they are available for you."

Việt Nam's Constitution of 1992
Article 51

1. *The Vietnamese economy is a socialist-oriented market economy with multi-forms of ownership and multi-sectors of economic structure; the state economic sector plays the leading role.*

2. *All economic sectors are important constituents of the national economy. Actors of different economic sectors are equal, cooperate, and compete in accordance with the law.*

3. *The State encourages, provides favorable conditions for entrepreneurs, enterprises and individuals, and other organizations to invest, produce, and do business, contributing to the stable development of the economic branches and national construction. Private possessions of individuals, organizations of investment, production, and business are protected by the law and are not subjected to nationalization.*

A dental implant is made of three parts:
the body, the abutment, and the crown.
The body is a hollow titanium cylinder
that most resembles a screw. It goes
up against the gums in the clear spot
between the two adjacent teeth. Six to
eight months after the body is installed,
the surgeon cuts back into the gums and
screws in abutment holders, which look
like metal nubs. This is what is visible
while the crowns are being made, which
takes about three weeks. Finally, the
crowns are fitted: the nubs are removed
and replaced with abutments, which are
also titanium with a screw body, but
which have angled, pointy heads that get
cemented to the crown.

As my tour continued, Mr. Aw and the Smiling Salesman walked me through the community and shopping areas. Directly outside was a cluster of landscaped swimming pools where families were enjoying the water and taking selfies. I could see Singapore from the pools which overlooked the Johor Strait. Many children were splashing around with their parents and their parents' parents—a picture of the multigenerational demographic Forest City seemed to desire. I could hear water splashing, children laughing, and footsteps shuffling around. When I followed the sounds of glee back to their source, I saw that from another promontory people were jumping off of zip lines, laughing carefree; beneath them, others were paddling canoes.

We headed indoors to another side of the glass building, which featured the model units. There were options: studio, one-bedroom, two-bedroom, three-bedroom.

The units were similarly and tastefully decorated, with distinct color palettes and a nice balance of textures. Living rooms had a leather sofa in light brown or light grey, a midcentury-inspired coffee table, maybe a porcelain tea set, some coffee table books on home decor, a leather ottoman, a linen armchair, an earth-toned striped rug. The kitchens all seemed designed for families or couples—in Forest City, no one lived alone. There were bowls of plastic fruit, plates of carved-foam cake, varieties of olive oil, and champagne for two. The dining table could be set for four or six, and all of the chairs were big, upholstered, and heavy. The bedrooms had plenty of storage space—walk-in closets, wood armoires, and shelves lined with picture frames of sample family moments: a child on a swing, a wedding, a father and son fishing in a small boat. The beds were piled with decorative pillows and, in one case, a swan folded out of a towel. Kids' rooms were outfitted with bunk beds, desks, stuffed animals, toy trucks, dolls, and alphabet boards. Bathrooms were marble and glass. The master baths had tubs with jets.

As I stepped out onto a model balcony, I was greeted by a grilling station, complete with plastic skewers and some plastic plants made to look like they were

growing off of the balcony. I turned to
the Smiling Salesman and asked him,

"How many varieties of plants will be
grown in Forest City, and what are they?"

"Many kinds!" he replied.

"What kinds?" I asked again. He said
he would get back to me.

All day I had been looking at tangled
and coiled plastic plants, and a few real
plants of the tropical-resort variety. Of
the plastic plants, I could count maybe
five different shapes; of the real ones, I
counted palm trees, bromeliads, chestnut
trees, and a handful of other short shrubs
and flowers. I did not see close to the
one hundred species of plants, as the
newspapers had promised.

As I left the model units, I remained
fixated on the art on one living room's
wall. I had seen a few similar pieces
throughout the day, but this particular
work was probably seven feet tall and
hung behind a TV screen that was playing
a Forest City promotional video on a
loop. It was a giant photographic print
of an autumn landscape in the Northern
US. In the foreground were some thick
pine branches. In the distance, enormous

grey-blue mountains with snow caps. Clouds sailed across the peaceful blue sky. There was a line of birch trees with golden yellow leaves. The top half of the landscape was reflected in a crystal clear body of water that extended all the way down to the print's bottom edge. It was a picture of another paradise, but not of the *King Kong* or *Jurassic Park* variety. This paradise was not anywhere close to Malaysia, and yet whatever the picture might mean in terms of aspiration and success, here, in the middle of a man-made tropic, it made sense.

Việt Nam's Constitution of 1992
Article 53

1. *The land, water resources, mineral resources,
   wealth lying underground or coming from the sea
   and the air, other natural resources, and property
   invested and managed by the State are public
   properties, coming under ownership by the entire
   people represented and uniformly managed by the
   State.*

A few weeks before phase one of my implant surgery, my teeth were scrubbed down, just as they had been when my braces were taken off. Dr. Fujishige's assistant snapped off the tooth-colored plastic attachments, the plaque was chipped away with a pointed tool, pumice swished around with an electric brush, and a special whitening medium was sprayed all over my teeth with a cold-air tube. By the end of it all, my teeth felt like smooth marble as I ran my tongue across them. I was ready.

Dr. Chen greeted me and then picked up a long Q-tip that had been soaking in a numbing gel. Within a few minutes, I was only half in the room. I could see what was going on, could even feel Dr. Chen touching my mouth, but everything felt gentle, remote. I felt two slight punctures through my gums on the right and left incisor gaps. "And you're done," said Dr. Chen. Not even 20 minutes had passed, and he had already sewn up my gums, now with new biocompatible parts inside.

After surgery, Dr. Chen's nurses took me to a dark resting area, seated me in an armchair, and wrapped me in a soft throw. I was surprised that I was not in pain. My gums were swollen, and it was a little awkward to eat, but not so much that I needed special food. The only issue was that my prosthetic teeth no longer fit. Until they did, the gaps in my gums would be exposed once again. So I hid at home for a week, waiting for my gums to shrink.

Việt Nam's Constitution of 1992
Article 54

1. *Land is a special resource of the nation, an important resource of national development, and is managed in concordance with the law.*

2. *Organizations and individuals are entitled to land assignment, land lease, and recognition of the land use right by the State. Land users have the right to transfer the land use right, and practice related rights and duties in concordance with the law. The land use right is protected by the law.*

3. *The State shall recover land used by organizations and individuals in imperative cases provided by the law for the purposes of national defense, national security, and socio-economic developments for national and public interests. The recovery of land must be public and transparent, and compensation must be provided in accordance with the law.*

4. *The State shall effect acquisition of land in cases of urgent demands which are provided by the law with respect to the implementation of the businesses of national defense, national security, and wars, emergency, and prevention and protection against natural calamities.*

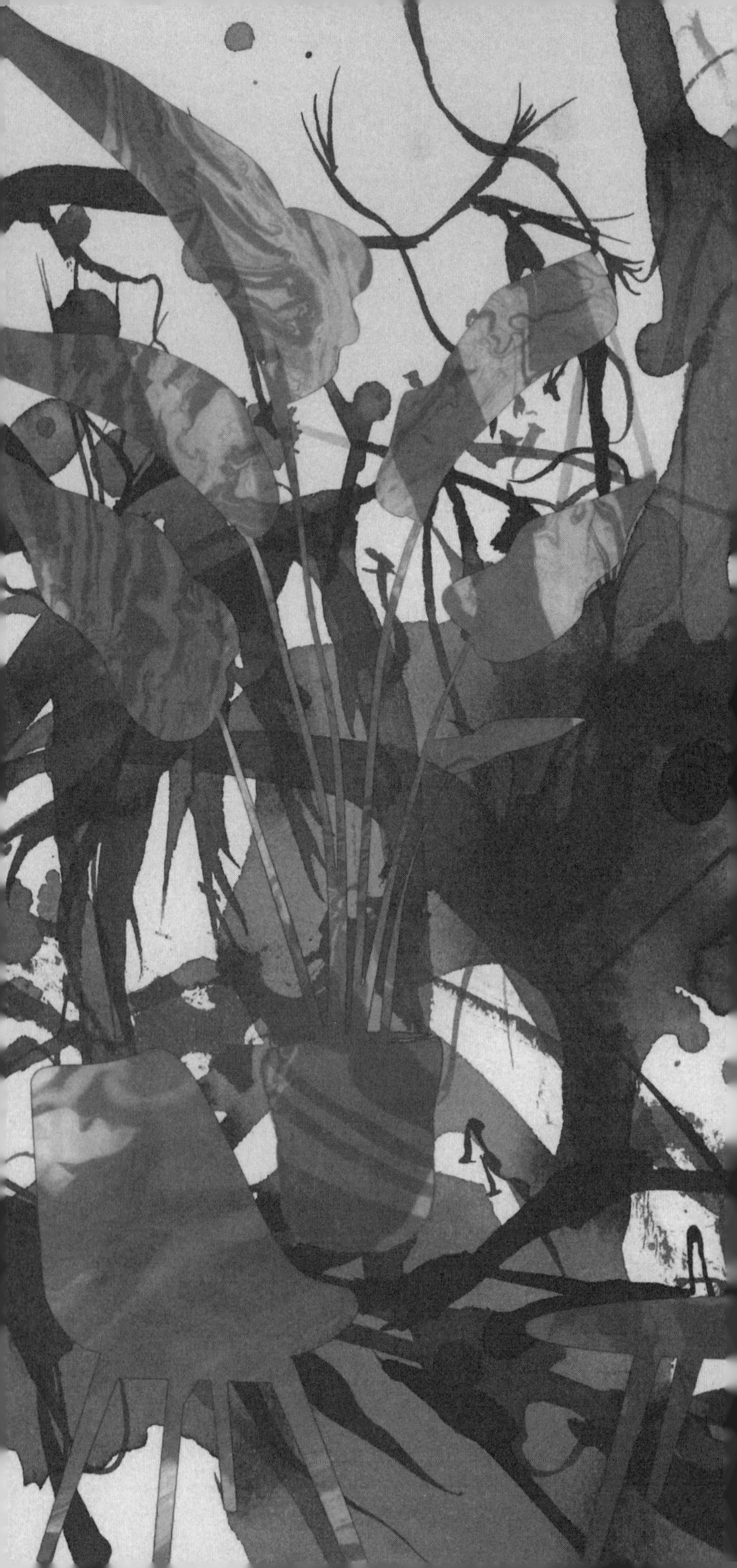

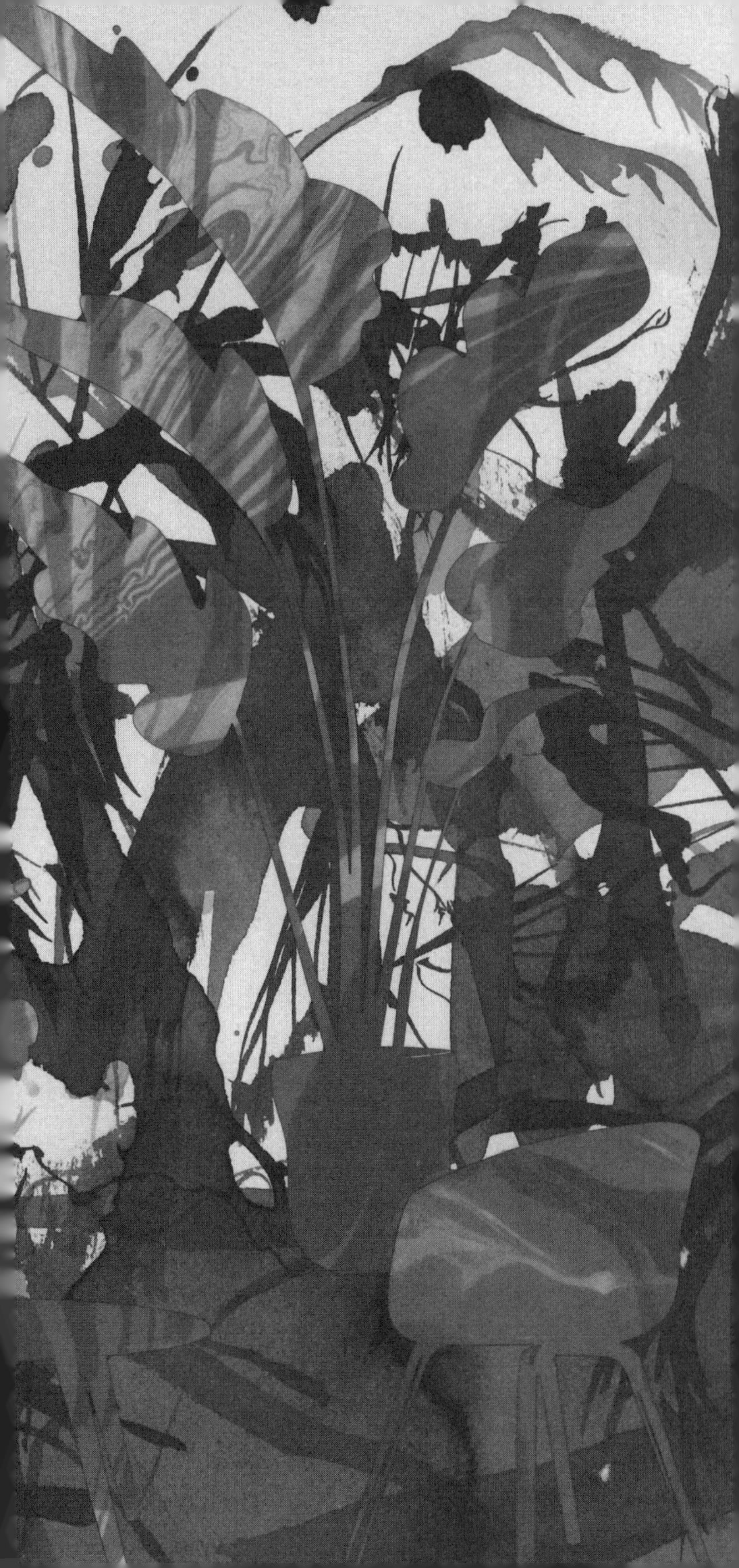

The Smiling Salesman sat me down at a lounging area and started to crunch the numbers. The smallest unit on Forest City, he explained, was 635 ft² and priced at 820,000 Malaysian Ringgits (RM), which came to just under $200,000. The next unit was 893 ft², priced at RM1,250,000, or $300,000. A 2,034 ft² unit was RM1,870,000, around $450,000, and a 2,917 ft² unit was RM3,010,000, just over $700,000. "Not bad," I told the Smiling Salesman, "well, not as bad as New York." Still smiling, he told me that if I were to buy then and there, I would receive a 20% discount, and that there were several payment plans which would qualify me for even more discounts. If I were to pay in full that day, I could walk away with a small condo in Forest City for around $150,000. I graciously shook his hand, and told him I would be in touch.

At the end of my tour, Mr. Aw offered to drop me at the hotel, just over the bridge on mainland Johor. "It is a five-star gold resort overlooking our new eighteen-hole golf course," he told me on the drive over.

We passed by piles of dirt until we reached the grand, looping entrance to the resort. Unlike the Forest City building, this building was mostly made of dark wood. The lobby ceiling was so high that there was enough space for the BMW 520d parked in the center of the room to sit beneath a giant gold sculpture that hung from the ceiling. "Everything is complimentary. Keep in touch, and tell your husband to come next time!" Mr. Aw said goodbye with a smile.

There was hardly anyone at this resort, except for the group of Hanoian ladies I had seen earlier at lunch. Now, they were lounging in bathrobes talking about the mud wrap they had just received. We were all enjoying the buffet dinner, which featured a spectrum of international foods: coconut curry, smothered shrimp, strip steak, iceberg lettuce, noodles. There was also an eclectic dessert bar with delicate cubes of tiramisu, blueberry cream cake, lemon curd, and fudge. I ate alone and went up to my room.

The room was enormous. I had a king-size bed covered with orange decorative pillows and a balcony that overlooked the sprawling golf-course, which was deserted. I could see one small crane in the far distance. I noticed a cluster of bats sleeping upside down in a palm tree. The sun was quickly setting, and the grass on the golf course was no longer visible. All I could see was the light from that faraway crane, which now looked a little bit like a bright white pearl. David Van would have loved this place.

While it takes six to eight months for an implant to become part of any human body, it took me almost a year to complete the implant process. This was mostly because I needed to find a block of days during which I could heal without anyone seeing me in the process—a day when Dr. Chen could uncover my implants in the morning and I could see Dr. Fujishige immediately after so he could adjust my prosthetic. This special day was a challenge to find, but eventually we found it: June 14, 2019.

I went to Dr. Chen's office for a short final visit. He took some x-rays, which were projected for me in a consultation room. Dr. Chen waltzed in and, within a few seconds of looking at the screen, exclaimed, "Yes! That looks good!" He turned to me, held my chin and told me to open my mouth. "Looks good," he said again. After he saw that I had healed well and that my body had accepted the implants, he proceeded to open my gums.

Just as in the first surgery, Dr. Chen began by dabbing some numbing gel onto my gums. After that he worked fast and efficiently. I felt a series of small prickling sensations, and then he was done. When I looked into the bright mirror, I could see there were round, shiny metal nubs sticking out from my gums. It looked clean but a little horrifying, evoking Frankenstein and other sci-fi imaginings. I felt light-headed but I managed to take the B train downtown to Dr. Fujishige's office.

I was mainly concerned with how I would get my prosthetic to cover these metal nubs for the next three weeks. Dr. Fujishige shaved down the plastic and the false teeth to fit around my new metal nubs. Then he made a 3D scan of my mouth and a plaster impression, along with several digital photos, all for the dental artisan who would sculpt my permanent crowns from zirconia, a ceramic material that is generally found in placer deposits—riverbed deposits of wind-worked sand, much like the sand left behind by the millions of years of wind that carved away at Phong Nha.

Three weeks later, my crowns were ready. The tiny little things were waiting for me in a black jewelry box in Dr. Fujishige's consultation room. "Okay, let's

see if this works! They have to be perfect."
he said with his usual cheer. He used a
tiny screwdriver to remove the metal nubs
from the tubular body of the implant.
There was a smell of deep body buildup so
foul that it made me think of death—like
the time my grandmother died, perhaps
like David Van smelled when they found
his body rotting alone in his house.

"Your crowns will sit half a millimeter
below your gums," Dr. Fujishige explained
as he twisted two pointy abutments into
the body of the implant. "We are going
to use a special cement that is really going
to make these crowns stick." He squeezed
out a gooey substance. In a few minutes,
the whole thing was done, the life saga
complete. The entire office's staff rushed
in and rejoiced. "They look real!"

My teeth were made a few blocks south-
east of Herald Square in New York at a
company called Creodent. I paid them
a visit to learn about how they made my
permanent crowns. At the office I met a
man named Reno, who took me on an
elaborate tour of the facility.

The Creodent floor of 29 30th St. in
New York City was bustling with activity—
not your idea of a quiet laboratory. A desk
with several receptionists greeted us, and
behind them I could make out multiple
rooms with people shuffling back and
forth between them. A melee of dental
equipment, tiny, small, and large, were
messily organized according to their use
in the different stages of the sculpting
process. There were areas for digital
modeling, casting, baking, and more.
Round swivel chairs were in a disarray.

Reno spoke to me in a thick Long
Island accent. "There's a lot I could show
you . . . I don't even know where to begin.
Follow me."

Creodent, I learned, creates false teeth
for use in many applications, primarily
dentures, bridges, and implants. Their
artisans work to model natural-looking

false teeth based on a complex portfolio of information unique to each patient. They measure the surrounding real teeth using cast impressions and 3D scans of each patient's mouth. Typically, the tooth is modeled in a 3D rendering program, printed in plastic and then hand-molded until a prototype is satisfactory. In the case of my implants, an additional "contact model"—a 3D print of my mouth with the metal abutments—was fabricated so that the teeth could be test-fitted perfectly.

There were teeth everywhere—on the artisans' desks, in the ovens, and in the bins that lined the walls, people's fake teeth shimmered in tiny planes of limestone, salt, and the silver-and-gold glitter of gypsum. In a narrow room with a row of computers lining one wall, Reno pointed to several screens where images of teeth spun around in 3D space. They were blown up to the size of the entire screen; I could see how even the teeth's false ridges were thoughtfully crafted to look like natural imperfections. Next to each computer and lining shelves that extended up to the ceiling were boxes and trays holding plaster and plastic models of many mouths. Each mouth likely had a story, I thought, but here, all together, they seemed like costume accessories.

The total cost of correcting my birth defect, including my childhood braces, was nearly $20,000. A month after the process was complete, swimming through one of the caves in the Phong Nha Karst, I thought about the final tally, about how insurance covered $1,200 because my condition was, in the end, deemed congenital. As I swam, the passageway became narrower. I had to listen for the sound of water trickling to find my way out. I opened my mouth and blew some O's into the water, letting some run through my teeth. As the water pushed through, the cold isolated itself on my front teeth, flooding my brain with a freezing sensation. But the implants on either side sat firm and unmoved.

This is how you create a vessel:

Form a ball of compressed clay by rocking a lump back and forth, constantly pushing it down on a hard surface. This will force all of the air bubbles out so that the clay remains the same consistency throughout and that the vessel does not explode when it is fired.

Seated at a potter's wheel, water in a bucket on one side and tools on the other, secure the ball of clay in the middle of the wheel so that it becomes a mound. Your whole body must align to this mound so that you have placed yourself at the exact line of symmetry of the vessel soon to take its hollow shape. If you were to draw a straight line up from the mound, it would cut your body in half.

Slowly, press the pedal which spins the wheel. As the ball turns round and round again, your hands come down from above like a halo over the mound. As if protecting this spinning sphere of clay, allow your hands to hover over the wet earth until it becomes a perfectly smooth mound, like the top of a wet sand dune on an airless night. Then push. Push. Push slowly inward from the edges of the dune toward the center of the clay, and the mound will start to rise.

At this point, you begin to pull—pull the earth up from out of the compressed round pile. Still aligned to its spinning axis, the mound becomes a cylinder. It moves around the wheel like a tiny tornado, even starting to hum a round sound, "*O- O-O-O-O-O-O-O.*" As your hands guide the cylinder, the earth becomes taller and taller. "*O-O- O-O-O-O-O-O,*" it continues to whisper.

As the earth spins, you will feel it pulling at your whole body. Your back is fighting to stay aligned with the spinning axis as your hands try to control the wet clay. Once the cylinder is at the height of your desired vessel, simply push your thumbs into the top surface. Drive your thumbs with purpose down into the center and then, "*O-O-O-O-O-O-O-O,*" the earth will open.

Depending on what the doctor might order, there are many different kinds of false teeth. The crown, which is the tooth part of the implant, could be made with PFM or PFZ—acronyms for "porcelain-fused-to-metal" and "porcelain-fused-to-zirconia," respectively—or "e-max," a trademark name for lithium disilicate. Each material has specific characteristics in one's live mouth, and they all reflect light differently, which can make them appear more or less natural.

Of the three materials, metal has been in use the longest. Years ago, a metal tooth would be cast from a model, and liquid porcelain would be used to coat the metal; the whole thing would bake at around 2000°F. Today, zirconia and e-max are favored. Both are significantly stronger than metal. Zirconia, a ceramic, is a white crystalline oxide of the mineral zirconium, which is both naturally occurring—it can be collected from coastal waters—and created as a byproduct of the mining and processing of titanium and tin. E-max, also a ceramic, is a processed combination of quartz, lithium dioxide, phosphorus oxide, alumina, potassium oxide, and trace amounts of other elements. Both zirconia and e-max can be ground into a fine powder and re-formed by baking them at 3000°F–4000°F. Alternatively, a tooth can be milled from a hockey-puck-sized disc of solid material.

Reno was holding a partially used zirconium puck as he explained this. It looked ghastly—a diseased rock sprouting an overgrowth of obscure teeth. "Once a base tooth is created," he explained, "the tooth is coated with liquid porcelain, just as with metal. This porcelain comes in an elaborate array of color categories, further separated by family: group A for reddish brown, B for reddish yellow, C for gray, and D for reddish gray. Within each family, the porcelain comes in a range of tones from zero to eleven, lightest to darkest. After the porcelain is baked, a ceramic artist will paint details onto the tooth—you know, like spots or stripes that people usually have on their teeth. The tooth is baked again and then one more coat of clear glaze is added before it is baked a final time. This final coating mimics enamel. It fills in any imperfections from the model and serves as a preventative shield against bacteria."

This antimicrobial issue is tricky when it comes to dental implants, which must be simultaneously anti-microbial and biocompatible. Titanium is one of the rare metals on earth that the body does not reject. Bone and bacterial matter can grow around it; the body will never push it out as it would with gold, silver, or porcelain. These minerals, on the other hand, naturally repel germs; their antimicrobial characteristics have, historically, made them ideal materials for the manufacture of mouth plates, crowns, and false teeth.

"So much to show you . . . what else?" Reno concluded his tour in the packing and shipping area. Boxes held tiny envelopes filled, presumably, with people's teeth. Creodent tries to create a tooth that is as natural looking as possible, Reno explained. This has a lot to do with how light is reflected off of a tooth which is created by the sum of all of the materials it is made of: metal, or zirconia, or e-max coated with porcelain and painted with glazes.

"You ever been to a club and someone smiles at you and their teeth are so bright that it's blue? Like, Lamborghini blue?"

Reno asked. "Well, those people have old implants that were made from plastic fused to metal. Your teeth were made using the most advanced technology we have today, PFZ—that's 'porcelain-fused-to-zirconium'—and it reflects light in a much more deceptive way. When you go to the club, your teeth won't glow."

My bilateral incisors, made out of PFZ and painted with A1-colored liquid porcelain in glazed stripes, match my natural teeth when I smile in the sunlight.

The earth I am pulling is porcelain, a soft, white, ceramic clay.

"O-O-O-O-O-O-O-O," the white earth spins and spins. Porcelain is made of two important elements: a mineral called kaolin, which must be fired between 2,200°F–2,600°F and offers the form some plasticity; and petunse, a stone that is admired for its strength and which also gives porcelain its translucency. Often called "white gold," porcelain out of the East has been prized by the West since the thirteenth century. It is no wonder that David Van saw a whole future within the hollows of these delicate vessels.

As the white earth continues to open on the spinning wheel, my hands continue to shape the vessel by guiding the clay upward, outward, and inward. It is a cup, a vase, a jar, anything that a vessel could be. It could hold water, a bouquet of flowers— or gunpowder, like the vessels on the Hồ Chí Minh Trail.

I have decided that my vessel will be a *xun*, a porcelain instrument from China that has been in use for more than 6,000 years. A traditional xun looks like an egg with a hole at the top, three finger holes

along the front, and two thumb holes on
the back. Use of the xun dates back to the
Stone Age, when it was believed to have
been invented by early Chinese hunters
who tied hollow mud balls to the ends
of ropes. When the rope was thrown,
the mud orb would pick up the air and
resonate. Since then, the xun has evolved
into an instrument used for everyday
music and Confucian rituals. Many have
thought it the embodiment of harmony
between heaven, earth, and man.

"𝒪-𝒪-𝒪-𝒪-𝒪-𝒪-𝒪-𝒪," I blow into my
xun. I can feel my breath warm my lips
as air passes over my porcelain teeth, out
my mouth, and through the thin spherical
walls of my vessel. Covering the holes
in different combinations, I am able to
sound a melody, "𝒪-𝒪-𝒪-𝒪-𝒪-𝒪-𝒪-𝒪."

"𝒪-𝒪-𝒪-𝒪-𝒪-𝒪-𝒪-𝒪," Đồng whistles.

"𝒪-𝒪-𝒪-𝒪-𝒪-𝒪-𝒪-𝒪," sings the Porter.

"𝒪-𝒪-𝒪-𝒪-𝒪-𝒪-𝒪-𝒪," comes the
wind from Phong Nha.

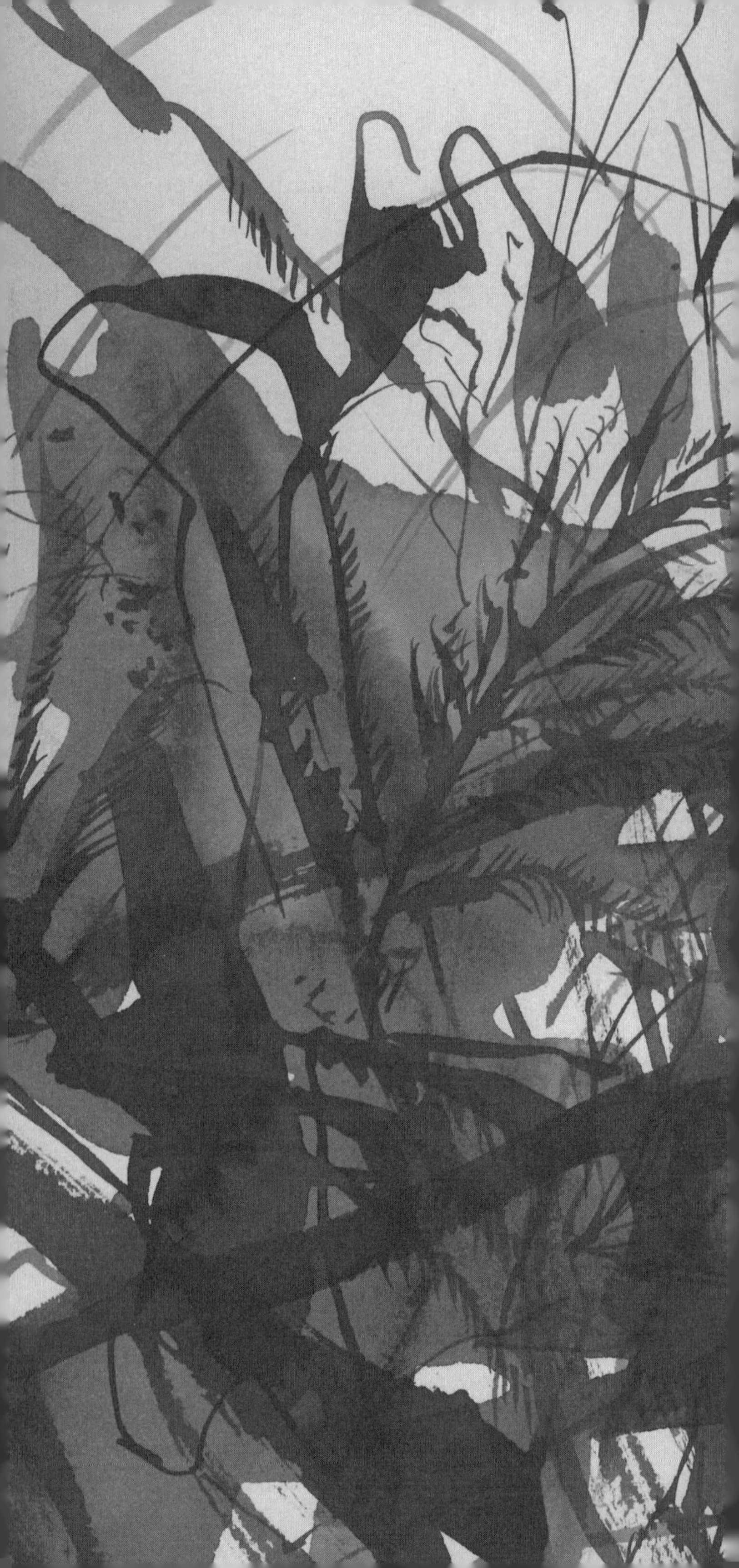

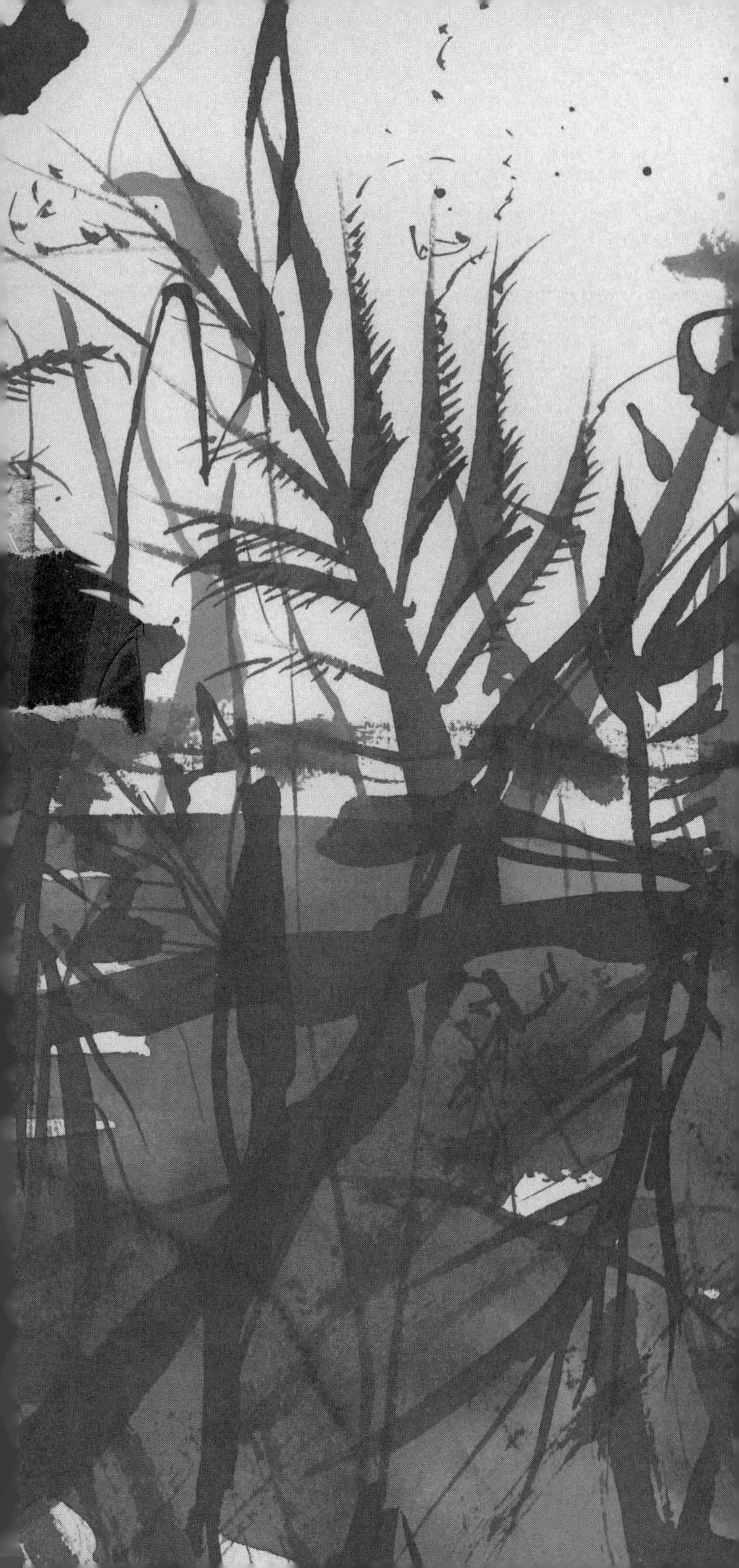

Socrates told his young disciple Glaucon to imagine a vertical line. "Now divide it in half," he continued. Glaucon nodded, and Socrates said, "Now divide those two sections in half." Glaucon did as Socrates said.

"There are two realms. The visible, which exists under the line, below the intelligible realm. The lowest form of truth lies in the first section of the divided line. Let's call this imagination. These are things such as shadows and illusion."

Glaucon nodded, attentive.

"Moving up the line, the second section, which is a higher truth than imagination, is belief. That's the world of physical objects—literally, what surrounds us, Glaucon, the fabric that covers our bodies, that tree over there, this vessel of water."

Glaucon continued looking at Socrates, nodding in acceptance.

"Now, we will move over the dividing line into the intelligible realm. Take a triangle that is equal on all sides. You know that such a triangle exists without actually seeing it. This is what we could call the realm of reason."

Glaucon quietly repeated everything Socrates said and then nodded in acknowledgement.

"Moving up to a higher truth, we reach the realm of *nous,* or knowledge: intellect. This is where reason transcends itself, becoming a form. Let's say, for example, I take this vessel and I pour the water out of it. Well, the water spills out because of gravity. This is a truth that humans know, not because it was an instinct, but because it was discovered through critical thinking. Or, let's look at that mountain over there. It's beautiful, isn't it? How do you know it's beautiful? Is there a greater truth to beauty, a truth discoverable through a process of thinking? Possibly—and this truth would be a form that transcends space and time. If the Earth were to end, the truth of beauty would still be true."

Glaucon looked over at the mountains. They had round, amiable peaks, with a dense forest that blanketed them in curls of green flora.

"But what do you need to understand all of this, Glaucon?"

Glaucon continued to look at the mountains. Glistening throughout the

jungle were glass buildings landscaped
with manicured flowers and plants that
hung off of rows and rows of balconies.
Like a grand driveway, or a gigantic lawn
to mark the importance of a palace, these
mountains were surrounded with miles
of rice paddies. Perhaps it was the time
of year, but these rice paddies glistened
with an electric green, the kind you
might see at a nightclub or painted on a
Lamborghini. It was strange to see such
green in nature.

"Light, Glaucon, you need light. Truth
is only possible because of the sun."

Glaucon turned back to look at Socrates.

"Let me tell you a story. In an ancient
time, three prisoners were chained inside
a cave in such a way that they could
only stare at the cave's wall. There was a
fire burning behind them, and behind
that fire was the cave's opening. Over
centuries, things would pass by the cave
and cast shadows onto the cave's wall. A
large mound that would often appear at
the center of the wall. Triangles with other
shapes stacked atop them would circle the
mound. One prisoner called these shapes
boats, and the other decided to call the

mound Island. Other times, when the mound disappeared, the prisoners would see a moving form constantly pulling rectangular forms from inside of itself and giving them to other moving forms. They named the giving form David Van, and the rectangles they called money. David Van would come and go on the days when they could not see the mound. Once, David Van had so many rectangles that the other forms stacked the rectangles on top of each other, and this giant rectangle the prisoners called house. One strange day, a giant shape rose out of the mound. They named this form King Kong."

Socrates continued: "The only thing the prisoners could see were these shadows. The prisoners would play a game with each other, guessing what shadow would pass on the wall next. Whoever guessed correctly would receive praise from the others and be deemed, for a time, the Master of Nature.

"But one day, a prisoner broke free and turned around. The fire that had been burning behind him was hot and orange, a color more intense than the orange he had been staring at on the wall. He walked closer to the fire until the heat started to make his skin sting. When the fire burnt him, he jumped away and looked up."

Glaucon leaned in, intrigued.

"When the prisoner looked up, he saw a long tube, something that reminded him of his own throat. Swallowing his own breath and spit, he gaped at the steep passage spanning hundreds of meters. It was filled with stalactites and stalagmites, protruding like overgrown teeth. He started to climb. For the most part, his movements upwards were triangular: left leg on a rock to the left, hands reaching at a point overhead, right leg following at an angled point to the right. And just like that, he made a steady course upwards and over."

Glaucon moved his fingers on his thigh as if to mimic the prisoner's triangular movement.

"Now, Glaucon, as I continue this story, I want you to remember that this tube the prisoner is climbing is precisely the divided line I had told you about. And the higher he climbs, the closer he comes to truth—to the good, which is the highest level of wisdom and knowledge."

Glaucon nodded, and Socrates continued.

"As he climbed to brighter patches of rock, he started to see that plants were growing. He climbed higher and the plants became longer and more prominent, many of them showing off large leaves. He could see that the bright round disc was not a disc, but a portal. At the highest rock, a blue butterfly flew in from the other side of the portal and rested on a leaf."

Glaucon sat up straight and slightly lifted his head, sensing a change in the story's direction.

"The prisoner finally came to the plane of the portal and stumbled through. The light was unlike anything he had experienced before. The light was a young spirit like a pure bright mirror. He squinted his eyes so his eyelashes could break the light, and he veiled his face with his hand. While his sight was a blur, his ears were alert to the noisy surroundings. He heard a bell in the distance and could see that people were gathered around two pieces of wood nailed together at a cross."

He heard water splashing, children laughing, and footsteps shuffling. As the light started to settle in his eyes, he took his hand from his face and saw, in the near distance, an enormous mountain. No one was near it; it loomed over the earth, rising so high that it almost touched this even brighter light that was floating in the sky."

Glaucon started to smile. He knew what the brighter light was.

"The prisoner looked around and saw that there were long lounge chairs and tables scattered around the area. The splashing water was coming from a cluster of swimming pools, and the children were laughing as they ran from one pool to the next. They leaped into the sky like eagles and flew down a long string until they landed on the water with big, friendly explosions."

Glaucon was a little perplexed as to where Socrates was going.

"As the prisoner watched the children, he noticed that each child had a shape similar to their body, which moved with them as they ran from pool to pool. He looked around and noticed that almost everything had a darker shape beneath it. A chair and a long table both had dark shapes beneath them, and these shapes shared outlines that were angled in

parallel. The prisoner saw that the table
was decadently covered in food. On its
right side, he saw giant prawns drenched
in a coconut peanut sauce, sautéed
cabbage, pasta with sauces, curry stewed
chicken, stir-fried beef, rice, a variety of
pickled vegetables, and a fountain of
Sprite. On its left, he saw coconut curry,
smothered shrimp, strip steak, iceberg
lettuce, and noodles. Further down the
table, he saw cubes of tiramisu, blueberry
cream cake, lemon curd, and fudge. As he
approached the food, he could see a dark
shape cast over it that moved with him as
he sniffed and examined each dish. He
looked back up at the mountain, and now
he could look directly at the bright light
above it."

Glaucon's mouth was salivating and
his body was tense with excitement as
Socrates continued.

"The prisoner realized that the bright
light was creating the dark shapes. As
he moved with his own dark shape, he
noticed that he could only see the shapes
when the bright light was behind him.
He looked at the big mountain and
then back at the cave's mouth, where

he had come from. 'It is not an Island, but a Mountain,' he thought to himself. Satisfied with his new knowledge—his new truth—he started to devour the food on the table. It was the most pleasure he had felt in a long time. The curry sauce gushed around his mouth, blueberries squished underneath his tongue, and he gnawed the steak off its T-bone. Then he heard a high-pitched cry: '*MAMA! SHE HAS NO TEETH!*'"

Glaucon's eyes widened in disbelief.

"Startled, the prisoner dropped his food and ran back into the hole, tripping, falling all the way down. When he landed on the dark floor, he found that he could no longer see the shadows, or his friends, clearly. Grabbing their legs for support, he tried to explain. 'Friends, it is not an Island, but a Mountain!' One of the other prisoners replied, 'What is it you're saying? What is a Mountain? That is the Island. Challenge us again and we will kill you.'"

Glaucon sat back, a little disappointed.

"And so, the prisoner wandered off to a dark corner of the cave where he could see nothing at all, not the flickering of the fire or the rays of the sun. Seated on the floor with his head between his knees, he started to let out a wail, 'O- O- O -O- O- O-O-O.' Meanwhile, outside the cave, the children splashed around, laughing. As the adults continued to lounge and eat, they would hear a sound coming from the cave: 'O- O- O -O -O -O -O -O.' They would stop for a second. Elders would whisper to each other, 'There are ghosts in that cave.' Parents would hold their children and say, 'Don't go in there. There are ghosts in that cave.' And so life went on. The people went on playing in the swimming pools and feasting on the food beside the mountain, never ever entering the cave."

FINIS.

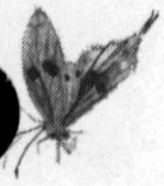